PIMLICO

62

THE ASCENT OF RUM DOODLE
AND
THE CRUISE OF THE TALKING FISH

W. E. Bowman (1912-85) was a civil engineer who spent his free time hill-walking, painting and writing (unpublished) books on the Theory of Relativity. He was married with two children.

THE ASCENT
OF RUM DOODLE

and

THE CRUISE
OF THE
TALKING FISH

———

W. E. BOWMAN

PIMLICO

PIMLICO

20 Vauxhall Bridge Road, London SW1V 2SA

London Melbourne Sydney Auckland Johannesburg
and agencies throughout the world

The Ascent of Rum Doodle was first published by
Max Parrish & Co Ltd 1956
The Cruise of the Talking Fish was first published by
Max Parrish & Co Ltd 1957
Pimlico edition 1992

© W. E. Bowman 1956, 1957

Printed and bound in Great Britain by
Mackays of Chatham PLC, Chatham, Kent

ISBN 0-7126-5479-8

THE ASCENT
OF
RUM DOODLE

To George and Margot

No criticism of any mountaineering
book or method, and no reference to any
mountaineer past or present is intended.

Contents

Foreword

by Sir Hugeley Havering, aisc, mpl,
Chairman of the
Rum Doodle Committee

It is with pleasure as well as with a sense of privilege that I associate myself with this account of the climbing of the world's highest mountain. The difficulties were many. They were overcome by the determination of each member of the expedition to give his best to the common cause. No praise is too high for these men. This is a book which should be read – and re-read – by every schoolboy and by all who value human endeavour and fortitude.

Introduction

by O. TOTTER

It is a pleasure and a privilege to associate oneself with this account of the ascent of the world's highest mountain. The obstacles were tremendous. That they were overcome is due to the dogged perseverance which each member of the team brought to the common cause. It is impossible to praise these men too highly. Every schoolboy should read this book twice, and so should everybody who honours courage and enterprise.

I

The Team

When I was asked by the Rum Doodle committee to lead the assault on the mountain I was deeply conscious of the honour bestowed upon me. To climb Mont Blanc by the Grépon route is one thing; to climb Rum Doodle is, as Totter once said, quite another. I hesitated to accept so great a responsibility, and only the insistence of the committee, particularly of its chairman, Sir Hugeley Havering, persuaded me to change my mind.

I would like at the outset to record my deep appreciation of the selfless devotion and sound judgment with which the Rum Doodle committee – and particularly its chairman – did its job. In no way was that judgment more effective than in the choice of personnel. If I had it all to do over again I would choose those same companions who supported me with such wholehearted and unselfish enthusiasm. I venture to say that no leader has been better served.

Our success was due to two things: magnificent team work and the splendid efforts of the porters, without whom the expedition would have failed.

In advising the committee on the composition of the team I had in mind a principle which has served me well on many occasions: to make one thing fulfil two purposes. Each member of the team was selected to be responsible for a particular organizational or technical job, and each had in addition some special quality which made him valuable as a mountaineer and a companion.

How well this policy succeeded will be evident.

The team members were as follows:

TOM BURLEY, Major in the RASC. In charge of the commissariat. Well known for his prodigious feats of endurance on many mountains, and chosen as our strong man. Had been high. Interrupted a mountaineering furlough in the Alps to join us.

CHRISTOPHER WISH, scientist to the expedition. Excellent on rock. Had been higher than most. Just returned from a successful first ascent in the Andes.

DONALD SHUTE, our photographer. Splendid on ice. Had been as high as most. Lately returned from the Rockies.

HUMPHREY JUNGLE, radio expert and route-finder. Had been nearly as high as most. Recalled from the Caucasus.

LANCELOT CONSTANT, diplomat and linguist. In charge of the porters. Chosen especially for his social tact and good-fellowship. Was expected to go high. Just back from the Atlas mountains.

RIDLEY PRONE, doctor to the expedition and our oxygen expert. Had been high enough. Barely returned from the Himalayas.

2

The Plan

After three hectic months of preparation we met in London, on the eve of our departure, for a final review of our plans. Only Jungle, who was to have spoken on the use of the radio gear and his own methods of route-finding, was absent. He rang up to say that he had taken the wrong bus and was not quite certain of his whereabouts; but he had just caught sight of the North Star and expected to join us shortly.

Burley, although not at his best – he told me he was suffering from London lassitude – gave us a detailed picture of the transportation arrangements. The object of the expedition was to place two men on the summit of Rum Doodle. This necessitated the establishment of a camp at 39,000 feet stocked with a fortnight's supplies for two, so that in the event of adverse weather conditions the party could wait in comfort for an improvement. The equipment for this camp had to be carried from the railhead at Chaikhosi, a distance of five hundred miles. Five porters would be needed for this. Two porters would be needed to carry the food for these five, and another would carry the food for these two. His food would be carried by a boy. The boy would carry his own food. The first supporting party would be established at 38,000 feet, also with a fortnight's supplies, which necessitated another eight porters and a boy. In all, to transport tents and equipment, food, radio, scientific and photographic gear, personal effects, and so on, three thousand porters and three hundred and seventy-five boys would be required.

At this point the telephone bell rang. It was Jungle, who seemed in the best of spirits. He had, he said, definitely identified his whereabouts as Cockfosters. We congratulated him and said we would expect him shortly.

Burley was congratulated on his masterly command of detail, although Wish expressed the opinion that the weight allowed for scientific equipment was scandalously small. He particularly wanted to take a mechanical glacier shovel and a three-ton pneumatic geologist's hammer, but neither of these indispensable items was allowed for. Burley was quite short with him. He pointed out that shovelling ice on Rum Doodle was quite a different thing from shovelling ice on Mont Blanc, while the rarefied atmosphere obtaining on the mountain would probably render the pneumatic gear impracticable. Wish burst into tears and said that he might as well go home at once, as he did not seem to be appreciated. Constant, in his tactful way, said that he was sure that Burley had no intention of belittling Wish's importance to the expedition; he had only meant that scientific gear was out of place on an expedition whose sole object was to place two men on the summit of Rum Doodle. This brought in Shute, who said he very much regretted the implication that scientific gear was a white elephant; one of the most important parts of our work would be the investigation of the effects of rarefied atmosphere upon three-dimensional colour television. Prone, who was suffering from a severe cold in the head, muttered something, which nobody quite understood, about 'ibportant bedical baterial' in a kind of enraged mumble.

Responsive, as a good leader should be, to human atmosphere, I sensed a hidden discord, and I quietly reminded all of the words of Totter: Mont Blanc might be climbed by a disunited party; Rum Doodle, never. This sobering thought had the desired effect, helped perhaps by the fact that Burley, overcome by London lassitude, had fallen asleep. Wish, who was to share a tent with him, was much distressed to find that he snored heavily, but he was consoled by Shute who reminded him that owing to the attenuation of sound waves in a rarefied atmosphere the snores would be much less offensive at high altitudes.

Wish then outlined the scientific programme. In addition to investigations into the hypographical and topnological fossiferation of the area he hoped to collect new data on the effect of biochronical disastrification of the geneospherical pandiculae on the exegesis of Wharton's warple. He also hoped to bring back a pair of each species of living creature found on the mountain in order to study the possibility of breeding mountaineers capable of living normal lives at high altitudes.

At this point Jungle rang again. It was not Cockfosters, he said, but Richmond. He had seen Cockfosters on a bus, but it turned out that the bus was *going* to Cockfosters. Owing to this he had, of course, set off in the wrong direction, but would be with us shortly.

After this, Shute described the photographic apparatus, the chief of which was a three-dimensional colour cinematographic camera. He hoped to obtain a film record of every aspect of the expedition's work. Suitable love-interest and accident sequences would be added by the company who had supplied the apparatus, and, with a patriotic song incorporated and the original material cut down to a minimum, the film was to be marketed on a world-wide basis as an epic of British heroism. If the summit were reached the successful pair would, if photogenic and under sixty, be offered film contracts for a picture entitled 'Tarzan and the Atrocious Snowmen'.

At this point a telegram was delivered. It read: SIGHTED BARKING CREEK NINETEEN THIRTY HOURS COURSE WEST NORTH WEST EXPECT SHORTLY WEATHER COLD BUT FINE JUNGLE. The postmark was Hounslow.

Burley awoke with a complicated gurgle and said that it was all wrong to clutter up a climbing expedition, the object of which was to place two men on the summit of Rum Doodle, with a lot of scientific rubbish. He expressed the opinion that a scientist on an expedition was even more of a nuisance than his gear, which was considerable. He told us about his friend Groag, who shared a tent with a scientist on the 1923 expedition to Tum Teedle. Like all scientists, this one was very absent-minded. One day he inadvertently made tea with copper-sulphate solution instead of water, with the result that he and Groag turned blue and were colour-blind for a fortnight, being unable to distinguish blue from white. One day this scientist stepped off the edge of a snowfield, thinking the blue sky beyond a continuation of the snow. He was saved only by great effort and devotion on the part of Burley, who had the misfortune to be roped to him. Burley said that any ordinary man would have left him to his fate.

Wish said that he did not believe one word of the story. He himself had drunk gallons of copper-sulphate tea with impunity. The blue effect was no doubt due to cardio-synthesis of the bloodstream due to the rarefied atmosphere. He strongly resented the statement that all scientists were absent-minded.

At this point a knock was heard on the door. It was a sergeant from the local police station. A policeman in Lewisham had discovered a furtive stranger loitering near the gas works. He had been found to be in possession of maps and navigating instruments and had been arrested as a spy. He had given his name as Forest and this address as a reference.

We gave the necessary assurances and asked the sergeant to transmit a message to the effect that we expected to see Jungle shortly.

Constant then told us about Yogistan, the country through which we must travel to reach the mountain. The natives, he said, were sturdy, independent people, friendly and of imperturbable dignity and cheerfulness. Their language, of which he had made a special study, was a branch of the aneroid-megalithic tongue. It contained no verbs and was spoken entirely from the stomach.

Prone said this was nonsense; if they spoke entirely from their stomachs they would suffer from permanent gastritis. Constant said that this was, in fact, the national disease, being hypodermic in 95% of the population. Prone said that if this was the case he didn't see how they could keep cheerful. Constant said that this was due to their strength of character. He said that he was not used to having his word doubted, and if Prone persisted in his present unco-operative attitude he, Constant, would have to issue an ultimatum.

Prone then spoke to us about the problem of maintaining the fitness which was so essential to our success. He urged us to follow rigidly the precautions which he had laid down, and handed each of us several pages of closely-typed manuscript. He said that if we followed his advice he could guarantee immunity from illness. Here he broke down with a fit of coughing and had to be thumped on the back. Constant did the thumping, and my impression was that he thumped a good deal harder than was strictly necessary. At any rate, Prone struck back at him, and a nasty incident might have ensued had not Prone been completely overcome by a fit of sneezing which made him quite incapable of defending himself.

I took this opportunity to thank all for their contributions, and remarked that I had no doubt that such little differences of opinion as might appear between us were evidence of the commendable frankness and openness with which we re-garded one another, and that I had no reason to suppose that we would not make an efficient and united team. I reminded them of the words of Totter: In an expedition of this kind the desires of the individual must be subordinated to the common cause. Constant said Amen, and on this solemn note we woke Burley and set about making our preparations for the morrow's departure.

*

Next day we sailed from Tilbury. As I stepped aboard two telegrams were handed to me. One read: BEST OF LUCK REMEMBER NOT CLIMBING MONT BLANC TOTTER. The other ran: STRANDED ABERCWMSOSPANFACH WILL FOLLOW BY PLANE SEND HUNDRED POUNDS JUNGLE.

3

To the Rankling La

The voyage was uneventful. My responsibilities as leader prevented me from spending as much time as I should have liked with the others, but I was gratified to see that the *esprit-de-corps* which is so important on expeditions such as ours was uniting our party into a closely-knit community. The importance of the team spirit cannot be overestimated. As Totter once said: when you are swinging helplessly at the end of a hundred-foot rope it is important to know that the man at the other end is a *friend*. It was this spirit, more than any other single factor, which brought success, and I was happy to see it growing during the voyage.

Humour was not lacking. Wish caused much amusement by turning up for dinner one evening with a black eye which he had sustained by walking into a davit, while on the same occasion Burley exhibited a bandaged hand injured during a game of deck tennis. Burley was down most of the voyage with sea lassitude, and it was a surprise to me that he had the energy for tennis. The others kept fit, except for Prone, who alone succumbed to sea-sickness.

Wish was kept busy with his apparatus. He tested our boiling-point thermometers and was able, by averaging the results of many readings, to fix the ship's height as 153 feet above sea level. Burley said this was nonsense, but Wish pointed out that due to the earth's not being a perfect sphere, but larger at the equator than at the poles, the result was quite in accordance with known facts.

Shute took many reels of film, but by an unfortunate over-sight he exposed them to daylight, so that no record exists of this portion of the journey.

Constant, to his great delight, discovered a Yogistani family on the lower deck, and spent much time with them improving his knowledge of the language. The association came to a sudden end, however, in a rather strange way. One quiet Sunday afternoon, Constant came running up the stairway in a state of terror, closely followed by a small but powerful oriental person who was waving a knife. After being rescued Constant explained that he had made a trifling error in pronunciation. He had wished to express admiration for the poetry of Yogistan. Unfortunately, the Yogistani word for poetry is identical with the word for wife, except for a sort of gurgle at the end. Being unable, in the enthu-siasm of the moment, to produce this gurgle, he had deeply offended his host, with the result we had witnessed. Constant kept to his own deck for the rest of the voyage.

One day a whale was sighted on the starboard quarter. This was naturally an event of great interest to all, but par-ticularly to myself as it enabled me to make up my mind on the very vital matter of the grouping of the assault party, to which I had given much thought. Our attack on the moun-tain was to be made by units of two men, who would climb together on the same rope and occupy the same tent. I con-sidered it important that these partners be brought together as soon as possible, to enable them to rub off those rough corners which become irksome at close quarters. I had, how-ever, been unable to reach a decision. Burley and Wish, I had decided long ago, were the ideal combination to fit into a cramped bivouac tent, one being large and the other small; and their personalities and interests were so different that there was little chance of professional jealousy or monotony arising. Shute and Jungle had each shown a lively and controversial interest in the other's special subject, and I thought it would be a pity to part them. Moreover, Shute was a Cambridge man while Jungle had been to Oxford, which would broaden the horizons of both of them. This left Constant and Prone; and I was not at all happy about these two – both having the professional manner, which might prove somewhat stifling in a small tent. But they disagreed so heartily on so many subjects that I began to be reassured, and the incident of the whale put my mind finally at rest. While we were leaning over the rail watching the creature blowing Constant said he wondered whether there was any truth in the Jonah legend. Prone said that he was surprised at such a remark from an educated man, and became so interested in the subsequent discussion that he forgot to be seasick. They argued heatedly for the remainder of the voyage and were quite inseparable, which was a great relief to me.

Just before we reached port I received a radio message: UNFORTUNATELY MISDIRECTED BUENOS AIRES SEND FIFTY MILLION PEONS JUNGLE.

*

The rail journey was uneventful. Burley was down with heat lassitude and Prone contracted malaria. Constant remarked that it was a good thing we had a doctor with us. I am sorry to have to record that Prone took exception to this innocent remark and was quite rude to poor Constant, but the latter generously overlooked this as being due to Prone's condition. Constant went into the native portion of the train to improve his knowledge of the language, but soon afterwards a riot broke out and he thought it advisable to retire. He explained that the natives were really friendly people of imperturbable dignity and cheerfulness, but they sometimes allowed themselves to be upset by trifles. We enquired the

nature of this particular trifle, but Constant said it was difficult to explain to a European. Wish spent most of the journey with a stop-watch in his hand timing the telegraph posts
in order to calculate the speed of the train. This worked out
at 153 miles per hour, but he thought that a certain amount
of experimental error should be allowed to cover irregulari-
ties in the spacing of the posts. Burley gave him a check and
found that the hand of the stop-watch had stuck. This caused
much amusement.

*

Our arrival at Chaikhosi was a big event, both for ourselves
and for the local people. Constant had arranged that the
3,000 porters should meet the train, so that no time would be
lost. As we pulled in we were surprised and gratified to see
that a great crowd, which stretched as far as we could see,
had assembled to welcome us. When we put our heads out of
the window we were greeted by a deafening cheer. Constant
remarked on the friendliness of the natives, which, he said,
was one of their chief characteristics.

As we stepped off the train we were met by a dignitary
whom I assumed to be the local Clang, or headman. Constant
engaged him in conversation, putting on his most diplomatic air. They spoke together for several minutes, and a
European onlooker might have been forgiven for concluding
that they were quarrelling violently; but I told myself that
this, no doubt, was the local idiom.

Finally, Constant told us that this was not the Clang at all,
but the Bang, or foreman porter, and that the multitude
before us were the porters he had ordered.

'If you ask me,' said Prone, 'there are a lot more than three
thousand of them.'

I was of the same opinion, but Constant said that nobody
had asked Prone and he was sure the number was correct.

'Why not ask your friend?' Prone suggested.

Constant engaged the Bang in another lengthy bout, after which he told us that the man spoke an obscure dialect and did not seem fully conversant with standard Yogistani.

'Let's count 'em, then,' said Prone. 'Line 'em up ten deep.'

Constant turned again to the Bang, and after much noise and gesticulation he explained to us that there was no Yogistani phrase for ten deep and, since military training was unknown in the country, the idea of lining up was not easily conveyed to the Yogistani mind.

I told Constant we would leave him to thrash the matter out with the Bang. He said it was a good idea; we were probably making the poor fellow nervous. As we left they went to it again, holding three fingers in the air and scratching on the dusty ground with sticks.

At the post office a surprise awaited me in the form of a letter from Jungle. He had arrived by plane three days previously and had gone ahead to break the trail.

*

We spent a hungry and uncomfortable night in the station waiting room, for until the dispute with the Bang was settled our equipment could not be unloaded, and in the absence of Constant we dared not risk a night in the local hotel. At daybreak I walked over to the train, to find Constant and the Bang still at it. The former explained to me that the Yogistani word for three was identical with the word for thirty, except for a kind of snort in the middle. It was, of course, impossible to convey this snort by telegram, and the Bang had chosen to interpret the message as ordering 30,000 porters. The 30,000 were making a considerable noise outside, and Constant told me that they were demanding food and a month's pay. He was afraid that if we refused they would loot the train.

There was nothing for it but to meet their demands. The 30,000 were fed – at considerable trouble and expense – and three days later we were able to set off with the chosen 3,000 on our five-hundred-mile journey. The 375 boys who completed our force were recruited on the spot. Boys are in plentiful supply in Yogistan; it appears that their mothers are glad to get rid of them.

*

The journey to the Rum Doodle massif was uneventful. We travelled along a series of river gorges deeply cut between precipitous ridges which rose to heights of 30,000 feet and more. Sometimes we crossed from one valley to another' over passes some 20,000 feet above sea level, dropping again to river beds elevated a mere 153 feet or so.

The steepness of the valleys was such that the vegetation ranged from tropical to arctic within the distance of a mile, and our botanists were in their element. I am no naturalist myself, but I tried to show an intelligent interest in the work of the others, encouraging them to come to me with their discoveries. I am indebted to them for what small knowledge I possess in this field.

The lower slopes were gay with Facetia and Persiflage, just then at their best, and the nostrils were continually assailed with the disturbing smell of Rodentia. Nostalgia, which flourishes everywhere but at home, was plentiful, as was the universal Wantonia. Higher up, dark belts of Suspicia and Melancholia gave place to the last grassy slopes below the snow line, where nothing was seen growing but an occasional solitary Excentricular, or old-fashioned Manspride.

The fauna, too, was a constant delight. The scapegoat was, of course, common, as were the platitude and the long-tailed bore. The weak-willed sloth was often met, and sometimes after dark I would catch sight of slinking shadows which Burley identified as the miserable hangdog. One afternoon Shute, in great excitement, pointed out to me a disreputable-looking creature which he said was a shaggy dog. Burley swore that it was not a shaggy dog at all but a hairy disgrace; but this may have been intended for one of his peculiar jokes. Burley's sense of humour is rather weak. He told me one day that he was being followed by a lurking suspicion, which was obviously absurd. But he is a good fellow.

We were naturally all agog to catch sight of the Atrocious Snowman, about whom so much has been written. This creature was first seen by Thudd in 1928 near the summit of Raw Deedle. He describes it as a man-like creature about seven feet tall covered with blue fur and having three ears. It emitted a thin whistle and ran off with incredible rapidity. The next reported encounter took place during the 1931 Bavarian reconnaissance expedition to Hi Hurdle. On this occasion it was seen by three members at a height of 25,000 feet. Their impressions are largely contradictory, but all agree that the thing wore trousers. In 1933 Orgrind and Stretcher found footprints on a snow slope above the Trundling La, and the following year Moodles heard grunts at 30,000 feet. Nothing further was reported until 1946, when Brewbody was fortunate enough to see the creature at close quarters. It was, he said, completely bare of either fur or hair, and resembled a human being of normal stature. It wore a loincloth and was talking to itself in Rudistani with a strong Birmingham accent. When it caught sight of Brewbody it sprang to the top of a crag and disappeared.

Such was the meagre information gleaned so far, and all were agog to add to it. The most agog among us was Wish, who may have nourished secret dreams of adding the *Eoanthropus Wishi* to mankind's family tree. Wish spent much time above the snow line examining any mark which might prove to be a footprint; but although he heard grunts, whistles, sighs and gurgles, and even, on one occasion, muttering, he found no direct evidence. His enthusiasm weakened appreciably after he had spent a whole rest day tracking footprints for miles across a treacherous mountain-side, only to find that he was following a trail laid for him by a porter at Burley's instigation.

*

The porters were unprepossessing. Mountaineering to them was strictly business. An eight-hour day had been agreed on, for which each received *bohees* five (3¾d.). Nothing on earth would persuade them to work longer than this, except money. When not on the march they squatted in groups smoking a villainous tobacco called *stunk*. Their attitude was surly in the extreme; a more desperate-looking crew can hardly be imagined. They were in such contrast to the description which Constant had given us that I was moved to mention the matter to him in a tactful way. He explained that they were used to living above the 20,000 feet line; their good qualities did not begin to appear until this height was reached. He said that they would improve as we got higher, reaching their peak of imperturbable dignity and cheerfulness at 40,000 feet. This was a great relief to me.

Their performance as porters left nothing to be desired. Although short – few were more than five feet in height – they were almost as broad as they were long, and very sturdy. Each carried a load of 1,000 pounds. One cannot praise too highly the work of the porters, without whom the expedition would have been doomed to failure.

The only one of them who was not worth his weight in *bohees* was the cook, whose name was Pong. Of all the barbarous three thousand, Pong was probably the most disreputable and the most startling in appearance. His face had a peculiarly flattened look, as though it had been pressed in by a plane surface while it was still soft. This same flattening seemed to have spread to his soul, for a more morose, unresponsive and uninspiring individual it would be impossible to imagine. His cooking was the reflection of his character. No matter what tempting delicacies he might extract from their tins the final result was an invariable and appalling dark-brown mess which had to be eaten with a strong spoon and contained the most revolting lumps. That we survived his ministrations must be considered a triumph of spirit over matter, for we suffered considerably from indigestion. All attempts to turn him out of the kitchen failed. At the least hint that we were less than delighted with his disgusting concoctions he went into a kind of frenzy and threatened us with knives.

The Bang either could or would do nothing to remove him. Perhaps they had trade union rules about it; however it was, we had to put up with Pong. No small part of our eagerness to get to grips with Rum Doodle was due to the desire, fast becoming an obsession, to get away from him. While on the march I indulged in long daydreams in which Burley and I, in a bivouac tent, cooked delicious repasts, while down below at Base Camp Pong writhed with frustration.

We passed through many villages, the inhabitants of which were invariably sullen and unfriendly, except when Constant made overtures, when they became hostile. He explained that they were not typical of the natives, being a degenerate class who, attracted by the soft living to be made below the 20,000-feet line, had become demoralized and lost their original qualities of dignity and cheerfulness. I may remark here that we came across no sign of habitation above the 20,000-feet line. This, Constant said, was because our course was away from the trade routes.

Shute was anxious to get a good film record of our progress. To do this it was necessary to start ahead of the rest so that he could set up his cameras in readiness for our coming. This simple plan proved more difficult in practice than he had anticipated. On the first three occasions he was unable to assemble his gear before we reached him, and it was as much as he could do to pack hurriedly and catch us up before evening.

Next day he made a specially early start and was not seen again until next morning, when he staggered into camp just as we were making preparations to move off. We had apparently taken different routes. This put him a day behind, for he found it necessary to make up for lost sleep. He did not catch us up until a week later, and then he went ahead and sat up all night to make sure of us. He shot the whole procession as it went past him, and everybody cheered. It was most unfortunate that on this occasion the three-dimensional camera should have developed double vision.

We were daily expecting to overhaul Jungle, although we had seen no trace of the trail which he had gone ahead to break. On the twentieth day we were overtaken by a runner with the following message: 'Captured by bandits. Send *bohees* fifty million ransom. Jungle.'

On the thirtieth day we received the following message by another runner: 'Repeat. Captured by bandits. Send *bohees* fifty million. Jungle.'

We concluded that the first messenger must have decamped with the money. After deep consideration I reasoned that I could place no reliance upon the honesty of these people, and I asked Prone, who was fully recovered from an attack of chicken-pox, to accompany the fellow. On the fortieth day Jungle reached us alone, bringing a ransom demand for *bohees* fifty million for Prone.

It was too much. I decided that the finances of the expedition could stand no more such demands. I therefore sent a trustworthy messenger with the following message: 'Sorry. Bankrupt. Contact Embassy.' On the fiftieth day Prone overtook us. Shortly after being seized by the bandits he had contracted double pneumonia aggravated by whooping cough, and had proved such a nuisance to his captors that they turned him loose. He was a pitiable sight: unshaven, with matted hair and staring eyes. His clothes were torn to ribbons and his boots had no soles. He was suffering from mumps.

Burley, who spent most of the day drowsing in a litter carried by porters, trying to overcome his valley lassitude, awoke one afternoon screaming. He had dreamt that the expedition was starving on Rum Doodle. He produced his calculations and checked them over carefully. It was as he feared. Due no doubt to his attack of London lassitude he had forgotten to allow food for the return journey. Concentrating as he did on the one objective of placing two men on the summit of Rum Doodle, he had forgotten to bring them back again.

I saw that this crisis would tax all my resources as a leader. I said nothing to the others, but carried my burden alone for a week, searching for a way out. At last I was forced to disclose the emergency. Wish gave one look at Burley – and I like to think that even in this crisis one of us, at least, was able to spare a thought for the unhappy author – and commenced to scribble on his thumb nail.

'The solution is quite simple,' he announced. 'Dismiss all but 153 porters and 19·125 boys. The food saved will see us through.'

This was found to be correct. Constant was asked to make

the necessary arrangements with the porters. The resulting uproar went on for a week, and Constant was in continual fear for his life. At last we simply could not afford to feed them for another day and were forced to pay them what they demanded, which was too much. The one bright spot was the hope of getting rid of Pong, but for some reason this did not prove practicable. Constant said he sometimes wondered whether the Bang had a vested interest in Pong; but this, I thought, was an unduly cynical view.

*

A month later we stood on the summit of the Rankling La facing the Rum Doodle massif, nature's last citadel against the conquering spirit of man. The great mountain itself, standing majestic against a cloudless sky, struck awe into the hearts of the puny creatures who were soon to set presumptuous foot on those dreadful slopes. What pen could describe our feelings as we viewed the Rum Doodle massif from the summit of the Rankling La?

I will leave the expedition awhile, paused on the summit of the Rankling La facing the Rum Doodle massif, in order to describe the configuration of the mighty mountain and the events which led to our presence on the Rankling La.

The mountain was discovered by allied airmen during the war. Several reports gave heights which varied between 30,000 and 50,000 feet. In 1947 a reconnaissance expedition was sent under Totter with instructions to locate the mountain, ascertain its height and investigate possible routes to the summit. Subsequent expeditions collected more information, but ours was the first serious attempt to climb the mountain.

The Rum Doodle massif is in the shape of a reversed letter M. The summit comprises two peaks: Rum Doodle itself and North Doodle. North Doodle lies to the west of the true summit. The various estimates of the height of the true summit vary considerably, but by taking an average of these figures it is possible to say confidently that the summit of Rum Doodle is 40,000½ feet above sea level.

The main ridge of the massif runs due north and south, broken by the watershed of two rivers, the Agenda and the Conundra, which divide the ridge into three portions separated by gorges some 20,000 feet deep. The true summit is situated in the centre portion, but North Doodle, although distant from it by little more than a mile, is separated from it by the Conundra gorge. From each summit a ridge runs in a north-easterly direction, the two meeting in a saddle known as the South Col (25,000 feet). The northern face of the South Col descends to the Rankling glacier, which winds around the south-east face of the mountain until it makes a sharp bend to the north-west. From the snout of the glacier emerges the Rankling river, which flows north after crossing the Agenda gorge some three miles below the watershed. The last stroke of the reversed M is completed by the southern ridge of the Rankling valley, which intersects the centre ridge of the massif at a point some two miles west of the true summit.

Our plan was as follows. Base Camp would be established at the head of the glacier at a height of 20,000 feet. Here we would spend some days acclimatizing. During this period reconnaissance would be carried out on the North Wall, which leads to the South Col. Advanced Base would be established on the Col, with an intermediate camp half-way up the Wall. From here to the summit camps would be placed in the most suitable positions. Our tentative plan was to camp at 2,000-feet intervals above Advanced Base, the final camp – Camp 7 – being at 39,000 feet, only 1,000½ feet below the summit. Each camp would be provisioned for a fortnight, allowing ample safety margin for bad weather.

The great question was: would the mountain go? Totter, in 1947, had written: 'The mountain is difficult – severe, even – but it will go.' Later reconnaissance had questioned whether the North Wall itself would go, but the final verdict had been that it would. Totter himself had summed up the prevailing opinion thus: 'Given team spirit and good porters, the mountain will go.' All the world knows now that it did. It is no small part of my satisfaction that we vindicated Totter's opinion.

But as we stood on the Rankling La we were awed by the mighty bastion which reared its majestic head against the cloudless sky. As we stood there, Constant spoke for all of us:

'She stands like a goddess, defying those who would set sacrilegious feet on her unsullied shrine.'

There was a murmur of agreement. In that moment we were humbled by the magnitude of the task we had set ourselves, and I for one sent up a fervent prayer that I would not be found wanting in the ordeal that lay before us. In such moments a man feels close to himself.

We stood there, close to ourselves, until sunset, the supreme artist, touched the snowfields of that mighty bastion with rose-tinted brushes and the mountain became a vision such as few human eyes have beheld. In silence we turned and made our way through gathering darkness to our halting-place in the valley.

4

The Glacier

Two days later we reached the snout of the glacier and commenced the long haul to Base Camp. Here we roped up for the first time. Jungle went first as route-finder, with Shute, who was to take films of us at some convenient point. With them were ten porters carrying camera and accessories. Burley and Wish followed. The former was suffering from glacier lassitude but was expected to acclimatize shortly. Then came Constant and Prone. The latter had developed German measles but was receiving the best of treatment at his own capable hands. The porters were distributed between the various parties. I stayed behind to meditate for a while on the responsibilities of leadership, and so brought up the rear.

The glacier was over a mile wide, deeply crevassed and littered with innumerable blocks of ice, most of them twenty to thirty feet high. The place was a veritable maze. Even the highest peaks were hidden from sight.

After some hours' march I was gratified to see in front of me the film gear, fully operational, with Shute at the handle. I left him to pack up his things with the help of his porters and carried on. An hour later I was surprised to see him once more, again turning the camera. I concluded that he had passed me without my noticing – as might easily happen – and was glad to congratulate him on his energy. He looked at me in surprise and swore that he had not moved from that spot since setting up his camera over an hour ago. I was about to remind him that this was neither the time nor the place for such witticisms when I was astounded to hear a call from behind. Imagine my amazement when I found that it was Jungle, who, instead of being out in front, had evidently dropped behind and been passed by the rest of us. Following him were a number of porters, in a long straggling line, and then, to our mutual bewilderment, came Burley and Wish.

I must admit that I was completely baffled. It was one of those moments when one doubts one's own sanity. I had, with my own eyes, seen the four people who were now with me set out ahead of me. Of these, I had passed Shute, who had nevertheless appeared ahead of me, while the others, whom I had not passed at all, were now behind me. It was too much to believe that we had passed each other in this complicated way without noticing it.

The question was: where were Constant and Prone?

It was Shute who supplied the answer.

'Jungle, you fool!' he cried. 'You've been and gone round in a circle!'

At once it came clear to me. We were stretched out along the circumference of a circle, everybody following everybody else. Shute had gone on filming us without bothering to identify us as we passed, and we had all gone round twice. If it hadn't been for him, who was the only easily recognizable feature of our route, we might have gone on all day.

Confirmation came shortly afterwards with the arrival of Constant and Prone. I think they must have been suffering from altitude deafness, for they were shouting at each other as though they were half a mile apart instead of only a rope's length. I congratulated myself on my arrangement of the party; two men who could carry on a spirited conversation after several hours' hard marching at 15,000 feet were obviously kindred spirits. It is one of the deeper rewards of leadership to find that one's manipulation of the human element has been successful.

I decided that the occasion was suitable for a halt, and over a glass of champagne we discussed the reasons for the mistake. I asked all to give their opinion candidly, without regard to susceptibilities. It is my belief that men are better friends for facing the truth together, and that evasion of any kind leads to distrust in the long run.

It was encouraging to hear how they responded to the appeal. Shute was particularly outspoken, and this, I thought, was a good sign in one who was to be Jungle's constant companion.

What none of us could understand was how Jungle, using his compass, as he assured us he had done, could have turned through a circle. The problem was solved by Shute, who made Jungle demonstrate his method. They wandered off together, and soon they, too, were discussing the matter at the top of their voices. Altitude deafness was, I thought, unusually prevalent that day.

When they returned Shute gave us the answer. 'The silly fool forgot to release the catch on his compass,' he told us. 'Naturally, it pointed north whatever direction he took.'

'It might happen to anyone,' I said. It is my experience that a man supplies his best when he is trusted. Nothing saps a man's confidence in himself so much as mistrust from those over him. It would have been fatal to the expedition to allow Jungle to doubt himself – to say nothing of the effect upon him in later life. I take no credit for my forbearance; such things are the essence of leadership; either one has them or one has not.

For this reason I sent Jungle off again after the break, confident that he would not make the same mistake twice.

Nor did he. After we had been on the go for about four hours I found the party at the edge of a vast crevasse – all except Jungle, who was in it. His compass had directed him to it, and rather than make a long detour in a doubtful direction he had insisted on being lowered into the crevasse, intending to climb up the other side by cutting steps. He had been down for two hours and nobody knew whether he was making progress, for his voice was multiplied by echoes and reached the surface as an undecipherable chorus. For all they knew he might be completely stuck.

It is in such moments of crisis that a man's real character is revealed. The veneer of manners and sophistication which enabled him to bluff his way in the civilized world is of no avail to him now. Unless he is heart of oak he will show some crack or blemish, some weakness which will betray him and his comrades. I am glad to be able to record that in this emergency each and all of the party emerged with flying colours. It is perhaps not too much to say that during the final stages of the assault, when things were as black as they could be and only character stood between us and destruction, the confidence engendered by that early incident provided the last ounce of effort which enabled us to win through.

Each, of course, met the crisis in his own way. Burley, with the *sang-froid* of a Napoleon, took the opportunity to recuperate his strength – sapped by glacier lassitude – by taking a nap. Wish was boiling a piece of ice over a primus stove in order to determine the boiling point of ice. Shute had detached the lens of his camera and was correcting it for the reduced refractive index of the rarefied atmosphere. Constant was improving his knowledge of the language by a shouting contest with the Bang. And Prone was treating himself for swollen glands, which he suspected to be incipient.

The behaviour of my companions on this occasion has been, I freely admit it, an example and inspiration to me on more than one occasion when panic threatened. I was both humbled by their calmness and warmed by the confidence which they evidently placed in me, upon whom the responsibility rested. They knew I would not fail them.

But time was pressing. If Jungle was to be rescued from his predicament before nightfall, something had to be done, and done quickly. Obviously, someone must go down after him; but who should it be? Thanks to the morning's incident I had the answer. To Shute alone should go the privilege of risking his life for his friend.

It speaks volumes for Shute's modesty that he did his best to concede the honour to someone else. But I could not allow him to forgo his real desire, and we soon had him dangling on a rope.

After he had descended some distance he disappeared from sight, and his voice became as incoherent as Jungle's. We lowered away until the rope hung slack, then awaited developments.

After some minutes it dawned on me that we now had two men down the crevasse without being a step further forward. Neither could communicate with us, and we dared not haul on the ropes for fear of injuring them.

The situation was desperate.

It was Burley who, waking up at this juncture, supplied the solution. 'Send down a walkie-talkie,' he said. 'We've carried the blasted things all this way; let's get some good out of them.'

It was a brilliant suggestion. Burley, I decided, must have the honour of descending with a radio set. Like Shute, he modestly declined the privilege, but I insisted. Soon he, too, disappeared from sight. I could have sworn that his last words were something about 'keep my ruddy mouth shut in future'; but this could not have been the case – unless, of course, it was another of Burley's incomprehensible witticisms.

Wish switched on another radio, and we waited breath-lessly. Nothing happened. A horrible suspicion came over me.

'Is the set in order?' I asked.

'How the devil do I know?' said Wish. 'Jungle's the expert.'

It was true. None of us knew how to use the radio. Jungle was to have instructed us at the meeting in London, but he had been unavoidably absent.

There was nothing else for it; Wish must go down. He would get Jungle to write down instructions, which would be pulled up by me on a line, one end of which Wish would take down with him.

Down he went; and up, in due course, came the message: 'Batteries not yet installed. Are packed in one of the loads, but Burley does not know which one. Send down champagne.'

This, I decided, would never do. Some channel of com-munication had to be opened. I scribbled a message: 'Please tell me what to do.' I wrapped this around the neck of a champagne bottle, tied the line round it and lowered it into the crevasse. I gave them five minutes to write a reply and hauled up the line. The message read: 'Send down an-other bottle.'

I hope I am not unduly harsh in thinking this an incon-siderate reply; certainly I might be forgiven for thinking so at the time. But, not wishing to appear dictatorial, I did as they requested, sending with the bottle another message: 'I earnestly beg of you to consider my position. All means must be used to extricate you from your predicament. Please advise at earliest convenience.'

Back came the following: 'Yours of even date to hand. Jungle overcome by vertigo. Absolutely imperative you send four bottles of champagne immediately, otherwise cannot answer for consequences.'

This, of course, put the matter in a different light, and I repented my quick judgment. I have since talked the affair over with Totter, who confirms my original opinion that the first message was not quite in the best tradition; but at the time I was anxious to make amends for my unfounded and ungallant suspicion that the request for the second bottle was without justification, and I thereby erred into leniency. That the message was justified must certainly be conceded; we – that is, Totter and I – question only the manner in which it was delivered, which made no acknowledgment of my own difficult position. But it is hard for me, who was at least on *terra firma*, to judge the feelings of those below. Perhaps I have, after all, been unfair to them; if so, I tender sincere apology.

I naturally lost no time in fulfilling the last urgent request, sending with the champagne another appeal for instructions.

The next message read: 'Jungle seized with convulsions. Send down Prone with five bottles.'

This worried me more than I care to say. It seemed to me that champagne was the last thing one would prescribe for convulsions. But Prone, who, sick as he was, pulled himself together manfully when I read the message to him and seemed almost lively for the first time in weeks, assured me that it was just the thing. So we sent him down too.

I gave them time to talk over the situation, then pulled up the cord. Up came an empty bottle, with this message round its neck: 'Bung Ho!'

At the same moment strange sounds began to issue from the crevasse. At first I could not believe my ears, but at last I was forced to the conclusion that my comrades were *singing*. Having some knowledge of British folk-tunes I was able, with some degree of certainty, to identify the music as 'Oh, My Darling Clementine', although, multiplied by echoes, it sounded rather like a full-size choir singing a kind of fugal Clementine. The result was not unpleasing, and I rejoiced that my friends had not lost heart; but unless they intended the song as a code message it was no help to me in my dilemma. I feared that although they were putting up a brave front my companions were in a situation of great peril.

This seemed also to be the opinion of Constant. 'They need me down there!' he said, and before I quite realized what he was about the brave fellow had pushed several bottles into his pockets, belayed the rope to an icicle, and was sliding out of sight.

Time went by, and the singing continued. I raised and lowered the line several times, but no message appeared. I was well-nigh desperate. Six human lives depended on my clear thinking and decisive action; but I was completely at a loss. My impulse was to descend the crevasse myself, even if it were to perish with my colleagues; but this would leave us with no means of communication with the surface.

The porters had long since settled themselves comfortably on their loads and were smoking the inevitable pipe of *stunk*. I could expect no help from that quarter.

Or so I thought. But I was to receive a lesson on the invaluable qualities of the Yogistani porter, without whom the expedition could not have been successful. The Bang, whose name, by the way, was Bing, suddenly rose to his feet and came across to the crevasse, bringing with him a small but immensely broad and powerful porter, Bung by name.

Without a word being spoken, Bung took hold of one end of a rope and was lowered by Bing into the crevasse. Hardly had the rope gone slack when a piercing whistle sounded from below. Bing at once began to haul in again, and you can imagine my astonishment and relief when Bung came safely to the surface holding Burley by his jacket with a mighty fist. Burley, dangling like a puppet, was happily singing 'Yo, Heave-Ho!' – as well he might.

It was too simple. One by one my companions were hauled to the surface, and a cordial reunion took place. I am not ashamed to admit that I shed a quiet tear. Jungle, carried away no doubt by relief at his narrow escape – although I like to think that some small part of his feeling was genuine affection – thumped me so hard on the back that I fell down; and Wish, who seemed a little light-headed after his ordeal, apparently thought it of the greatest urgency that he should inform me that he had measured the depth of the crevasse, which was exactly 153 feet. This seemed to him, for some reason, excruciatingly funny.

When all but Constant had been safely restored to *terra firma* Bing and Bung went back to their comrades. They had evidently forgotten Constant, or were, perhaps, unable to count up to seven. I went over to them and endeavoured to indicate by signs what I wished them to do. I was met by blank scowls. Their meagre intelligence was evidently incapable of grasping my meaning. I lined the rest of the team up, leaving a gap in the middle, and pointed to this gap and to the crevasse, then went through the motions of lowering and raising a rope and greeting a companion saved from the abyss. All nodded encouragingly – a few even applauded – but no one made a move. I went through the whole performance again; this time they took not the slightest notice, but puffed away at their *stunk* as if everything were normal.

The team had clasped each other around the shoulders and, still in line, capered sideways on the ice like a row of chorus girls, singing 'Don't Put Your Daughter On The Stage, Mrs Worthington'. Poor fellows, they were still slightly hysterical from the effects of their ordeal.

I was on the point of unmanly panic when Bing got to his feet, came over to me, leered in a most objectionable fashion into my face and scratched the palm of one hand with the forefinger of the other. He did it in a most deliberate and odious way, as though the act had some esoteric significance.

It was horrible. I honestly thought for a moment that he was trying to bewitch me. One never knows what goes on in the heads of such primitive people. After all, this was the Mysterious East; who knew what might not happen?

The others stopped dancing and gathered round. I appealed to them for advice. What should I do?

It was Burley who told me, although how he came to know about it I cannot imagine.

"Grease it, old boy," he said; "grease it."

I looked at him in astonishment. What was I to grease, and why?

Luckily, Burley took charge. To my amazement he produced a *bohee* ($\frac{3}{4}d$.) and offered it to Bing. The latter shook his head and scratched harder at his palm. Burley added another *bohee*, with the same result.

It seemed to me exactly as if they were bargaining over the price of something. Constant has since explained the matter to me. It appears that the number six is sacred to the Yogistani. Every sixth occurrence of a thing is treated in a special way. The sixth day is a day of rest. The sixth son is put to the priesthood. The sixth pipeful of *stunk* is smoked in honour of one's grandfather; and so on. The prescribed ritual may, however, be waived provided that a suitable offering is made to the gods. In this particular case, five lives had been saved; the gods had been deprived of the presence of five Europeans. To deprive them of a sixth would be the grossest sacrilege, and only a heavy monetary offering could adjust the matter.

The bargaining went on for some time. The Bang was evidently a devout person, for he upheld staunchly the rights of his gods. The final figure was *bohees* a thousand (£3. 2s. 6d.). Payment was made, and the Bang went to the crevasse, taking Bung with him. But this move did not appear to be popular with the rest of the porters, who had been gesticulating and shouting during the bargaining. They now rushed after Bing and Bung and surrounded them; and everybody began to yell at the top of his voice.

The argument went on for some minutes. Evidently, the porters were against the rescue; their superstitious minds were no doubt still uneasy, in spite of the handsome offering.

At last, to our great relief, the Bang appeared to be getting the upper hand. Soon the hubbub was quietened to a mild uproar and the two rescuers forced their way through the mob. In no time at all Constant was restored to us, none the worse for his adventure except for a distressing attack of hiccups. I now realized that it was past time to halt for the night, and gave the order to make camp. We turned in a happy and united party.

Some time in the small hours I awoke with a faint suspicion that there were undercurrents to this episode. Why, for instance, had the dramatic rescue taken place only when it was too late for further marching? I put away such ignoble thoughts at once, and mention them only as evidence of the deterioration which sets in at high altitudes due to the rarefied atmosphere.

*

Next morning no one was fit to travel. Burley, in reaction from his magnificent effort of the day before, had gone down again with glacier lassitude, and Prone was prostrate with a sharp attack of pins and needles. The others complained of glacier depression and pressed Prone to prescribe champagne. But the latter was, unfortunately, too ill to attend to them, and I dared not on my own initiative take the responsibility of administering so potent a medicine.

I need hardly say that champagne was carried for medicinal purposes only.

I was anxious to push on to Base Camp. We were already behind in our programme. Moreover, we were still on the glacier, and at any moment a crevasse might open beneath our feet, precipitating us into the abyss. I therefore gave the order to strike camp.

My companions were hoisted on to the backs of stalwart porters, and even I, feeling somewhat overcome by recent emotional experiences, allowed myself to be transported in the same way. Bing, the Bang, who had shown initiative in the crevasse incident, was sent ahead as route-finder. The day passed without incident. I awoke at noon to find the vast precipice of the North Wall towering above us. We were at Base Camp.

5

Base Camp

At Base Camp we set about the task of preparing ourselves for the job ahead. Our first concern was to acclimatize. The problem of getting the best out of the members of such an expedition is always one of the most difficult which a conscientious leader must face. It is threefold, and may be discussed under the headings: fatigue, acclimatization and illness. The question of fatigue is two-fold: if a man is overworked he becomes tired; if he is underworked he becomes lazy. The question of acclimatization is three-fold: first, a man must spend some time high before he is able to work effectively. Second, if he stays high too long he deteriorates. The effect of being high is thus very similar to that of being in a sleeping-bag. Third, if he goes low he will probably be able to recuperate. The whole thing is complicated by the psychological factor; and on this score I have but one rule: a contented climber is a good climber.

Thanks to the splendid work of Prone the expedition was remarkably free from illness. All were fit and well, except poor Burley, who had fallen victim to Base Camp lassitude and consequently was not acclimatizing as quickly as the others, and Prone, who was smitten with mysterious and complicated symptoms, namely: pallor, profuse sweating, pulse rapid and soft, temperature sub-normal, deep breathing and sighing, restlessness and thirst, cold extremities, faintness, dizziness and buzzing in the ears. Poor fellow, he was much distressed, both by his condition and by the fact that he was unable to diagnose his ailment. The problem was finally solved by Constant, who produced a first-aid manual and pointed out that the symptoms were exactly those of hae-morrhage, except that the last two were missing, namely: insensibility and death. He said there was still hope. Prone then discovered that he had cut himself in the ear while shaving and was slowly bleeding to death. After stopping the bleeding by holding ice against his ear and afterwards treating himself for surgical shock and a frostbitten ear, he went down with Italian measles.

The days of acclimatization were spent according to the character and duties of the individual. Burley superintended, as well as his condition would allow, the unpacking and repacking of the stores and, in his more active moments, evading the scientific attentions of Wish, who insisted on subjecting him, as the heaviest man of the party, to a harrowing process known as a fatigue test.

Wish was fully occupied with research of various kinds. At almost any time of day he could be seen shovelling or drilling the ice of the glacier, taking thermometer readings at various strategic points, hitting rocky outcrops with hammers, or calibrating his boiling-point thermometers. He offered a prize of $1\frac{1}{2}$d. for every specimen of creature brought to him, and 3d. for every Wharton's warple; but although we spent much time poking into crevasses and lifting stones none of us was able to supplement his income. Wish chose me, the lightest of the party, as his second subject for the fatigue test. Being anxious to encourage every aspect of the expedition I did my best to satisfy his demands, but I became so exhausted that I had little energy to spare for the others, which was rather unfair; but no complaints were heard, which was a tribute to the prevailing team spirit.

Shute took the opportunity to give his gear a thorough

try-out. His favourite test-piece was myself running up and down the hill which Wish had chosen for his fatigue test. I could only hope that these sequences would not be given, in the final film, the emphasis which they received at the time.

Jungle's job was to prepare the walkie-talkie apparatus and to instruct us in its use. I have always had a horror of electrical gadgets and I was relieved to find that our sets were quite simple to operate, besides being too weak to hurt us. But although the gear was simple the method of using it was not. In my ignorance I thought that we would call each other up as one does on the telephone. But it is much more complicated than that. In the first place, you never address a person by his real name. Code names are used. Jungle gave us our code names, which were as follows:

BURLEY: Deadweight	CONSTANT: Applecart
WISH: Fiddler	PRONE: Ailing
SHUTE: Dickie-bird	MYSELF: Binder

There was some argument about Jungle's code name. He himself had picked 'Pathfinder', but this, for some reason, proved unpopular with the others. Shute, rather tactlessly I thought, suggested that 'Pathloser' would be more appropriate. Eventually we compromised with 'Wanderer', but Jungle seemed hurt.

Then we had to learn the language. One must never, under any circumstances, speak in the normal manner. To say, for instance, 'yes', 'no' or 'very well' is quite unheard-of. Instead, one must use such expressions as 'that is correct', 'can do', 'will do', 'Roger', and so on. Two o'clock becomes 'fourteen hundred hours' and midnight, for some obscure mathematical reason, must never be referred to. To go East is to 'proceed zero-niner-zero', and 20,000 feet becomes 'angels twenty'.

There was also an elaborate ceremonial to be observed when calling up and replying. Finally, we were forbidden to use our ordinary voices; we must speak in a kind of chant which would make it difficult to tell one voice from another.

The younger members seemed to get a good deal of innocent fun from this ritual, but I must confess that I found it a little confusing.

The radio sets were made small to save weight, and their range was limited. It might sometimes be necessary to have messages relayed via one or two intermediaries. In view of certain youthful experiences at children's parties I decided that some practice was advisable. I asked the party to form a large circle over the whole width of the glacier, so that messages could be sent right round. At first I was quite unable to think of a message. My brain seemed to have frozen, and I stood for some minutes feeling foolish. At last, I managed somehow to compose the first message: 'How serene is Rum Doodle in the morning light.'

This came back as 'Binder's butter beans.'

After some thought I sent out the following: 'Please pay very careful attention to the message.' This, too, came back as 'Binder's butter beans.'

This was absurd. As an experiment I sent out: 'Binder's butter beans.' This returned as: 'The voice of the leader is sweet music in the ears of the followers.'

This sort of thing went on all morning. I was determined not to give up until we had mastered the technique, and greatly to my delight the messages began coming through perfectly, without any apparent reason for the change, just before lunch time.

By great coincidence we had butter beans for lunch, which I thought rather amusing.

Some of us were inclined to be sceptical about the value of

the radio; but we were shortly to receive striking proof of its usefulness. I was taking a walk one morning by myself, in order to meditate on the responsibilities of leadership, when my walkie-talkie began to buzz. I put it to my ear and heard a voice:

'Applecart to Binder. Applecart to Binder. Are you receiving me? Over.'

I flicked the switch to 'transmit' and said: 'Binder to Applecart. Binder to Applecart. Receiving you loud and clear. Are you receiving me? Over.'

Back came the reply: 'Applecart to Binder. Receiving you strength eight. Turn up two notches. Over.'

I turned up two notches and said: 'Binder to Applecart. Have turned up two notches. Are you receiving me? Over.'

'Applecart to Binder. Receiving you loud and clear. Good-morning. Do you know where corkscrew is? Over.'

'Binder to Applecart. Please say again. Over.'

'Applecart to Binder. I say again. Receiving you loud and clear. Good-morning. Do you know where corkscrew is? Over.'

'Binder to Applecart. Good-morning. Corkscrew is in right-hand pocket of spare trousers. Over.'

'Applecart to Binder. Roger. Over and out.'

One wonders how earlier expeditions managed at all without the boon of radio.

*

Constant had the job of paying off the redundant porters and instructing the remainder in their future duties. We retained 88 porters and 11 boys for the return journey, the rest being dismissed. Of the 99, those who were not actively employed on the mountain were to move Base Camp to another position where it would be safe from avalanches. Constant considered that they could be left to do the job themselves, as he had made everything quite clear to them. This was a relief to me, as every available European would be needed on the mountain.

*

I have made a special study of the effects of rarefied atmosphere on human behaviour, and had asked the others to tell me of any unusual experiences which might occur to them on the mountain. Even at the comparatively moderate height of Base Camp altitude effects were already perceptible. During an impromptu game of cricket Burley swore at the umpire – a thing which could never happen at sea level – while Wish showed a tendency to take more than his share of marmalade. But these were temporary effects which would disappear with acclimatization.

It was interesting to notice how the diverse characters of my companions influenced their choice of literature. Burley whiled away his hours of lassitude with *Bulldog Drummond*. Wish could be found almost any evening huddled over a melting block of ice reading *Martians and Atom Men*. Shute relaxed with *Three-Dimensional Murder*. Jungle displayed an unexpectedly romantic soul with *Love in the Labyrinth*, while Prone was never to be seen without a copy of his own work, *The Secret of Radiant Health*, except when he had mislaid it.

My duties did not allow of frivolous relaxation. But it is worth recording that Bing, the Bang, spent much of his leisure immersed in a Yogistani translation of *Three Men in a Boat*.

We foregathered in the evening for a social hour, and many a spirited discussion took place at these gatherings. On one occasion we discussed the old question: should oxygen and other artificial aids be used on mountains. Burley said that it was a lot of ruddy lumber; more trouble than it was worth. He told us about his friend Baffles, who carried an oxygen set weighing forty pounds to the summit of Mi Wurdle, only to find when he got there that the apparatus had been out of order all the time. Wish said that this remark was typical of the layman's ignorant point of view. We had a unique opportunity to test our gear under rigorous conditions, and our duty was to do so. He asked Burley why, if he disagreed with its use, he was willing to use it. Burley asked whether Wish expected him to climb the ruddy mountain naked. Wish said that this was a typically unscientific argument. He said he had long been aware that to some the ascent of the mountain partook of the frivolous nature of a sporting event. He himself took a sterner view. To him, the climax of our efforts would be the fulfilment of his own self-dedicated task of determining the melting-point of ice on the summit. He reminded Burley that without oxygen the exacting intellectual efforts which this delicate experiment demanded would be quite impossible. Burley, rather tactlessly I thought, said that, speaking with wide experience and an excellent memory, he could recall nothing which approached this for futility. He said that nobody except a demented scientist would want to melt ice on the tops of mountains, and even if he did, who cared what the temperature was? He told us about his friend Strokes, who had had the ice melted under his feet by a scientist on the summit of the Schmutzigstein and had lost three toes in consequence. He said that any scientist was a menace on a mountain.

While they were arguing this point with their usual commendable frankness Shute said that without artificial aids the taking of three-dimensional films would also be impossible; and this prompted Jungle to remark that that was sufficient justification for doing without them. His own motive in climbing was to escape from mechanical civilization and everything that it stood for, especially films. Constant said that he deplored the narrow outlook of the others. *He* climbed solely to demonstrate the triumph of the spirit over adverse circumstances. He said that artificial aids were unsportsmanlike; if they were carried to their logical extreme we might find climbers impaling the summit of a mountain with a long-range harpoon attached to a rope ladder. If summits could not be climbed unaided they were better left unclimbed. Prone said this was rubbish; if artificial aids were refused tents and clothing must go with them. He asked Constant if his triumphant spirit was prepared to climb Rum Doodle in a loin cloth, or worse.

Although I believe in plain speaking between friends I really felt that it was being overdone on this occasion. I therefore reminded all of the words of Totter on the subject: no practical mountaineer would refuse the help of science, but there are limits. I expected this to put an end to the discussion – for what more is there to say? – but nobody seemed to take any notice. It was obvious to me that we were still suffering from the rarefied atmosphere.

6

North Wall : the First Assault

At last, all were considered acclimatized, with the exception of Prone, who had developed blood-pressure; and we set out to assault the North Wall. I sent off the following message by runner: 'Moving to attack North Wall, the tremendous precipice which rears above us 5,000 feet against the sky. The question on all lips is: "Will it go?" and every heart whispers a confident: "Yes, it will!" The spirit of the team is excellent and the porters are beyond praise. All in good health.'

The North Wall is a sheer glass-like face of ice broken only by rock, snowfields, ice-pinnacles, crevasses, *bergschrunds*, ridges, gulleys, scree, chimneys, cracks, slabs, *gendarmes*, *Dames Anglaises*, needles, strata, gneiss and gabbro. A formidable obstacle, and one to daunt the hearts of a disunited party supported by mediocre porters. Our plan was to establish Advanced Base on the South Col, which is immediately above the North Wall; but it was expected that one intermediate camp would be needed.

We had already reconnoitred the lower slopes of the wall, and two schools of thought had arisen concerning the best method of tackling it. Wish, our cragsman, favoured the direct ascent of a precipitous rock-face which led to what seemed easy going higher up. Shute, the ice expert, preferred a steep slope of ice which likewise appeared to ease off towards its upper extremity. Since no final decision was possible it had been decided to try both ways simultaneously.

Shute and Jungle would tackle the ice, Wish and Burley would attack the rock. Constant and I, after tidying up at Base, would follow on to support either party.

Constant and I moved off shortly after midday, and we had not yet left the glacier when my radio buzzed. It was Jungle in a high state of excitement. Shute was stuck half-way up his ice-field, having lost his ice-axe and being afraid to come down. Jungle's own axe was sunk in the ice with the rope belayed to it. He dared not remove it in case Shute should fall. Would we please come and help him?

This was alarming news. I immediately assured Jungle that we would be with him as quickly as possible, and we set off at full speed. But we had gone no more than a few paces when Constant disappeared into a crevasse. The rope tightened between us and I was jerked on to my face. In the excitement I let go of my ice-axe and found myself being pulled towards the lip of the crevasse with no means of stopping myself. I was within two yards of the edge when I stopped. The rope had cut into the ice and the increased friction had saved me.

But it was a desperate situation. When I tried to rise the rope pulled me forward as Constant fell still further. Only by lying spreadeagled could I get sufficient friction to halt his fall. I could do nothing to save Constant; unless help came there was no hope for us.

Our only chance was the radio. With my heart in my mouth I edged my right hand nearer and nearer, and at last I was able to place the apparatus near my face. I called up Burley and Wish. The former replied, and I asked him to hurry to our help.

To my consternation he informed me that they, too, were in difficulties. Wish was stuck half-way up his rock-face, being unable to move up or down. Burley was completely exhausted; evidently he had not fully acclimatized. He had himself been on the point of calling for help.

There was only one solution. Jungle must leave Shute, who at least was belayed to Jungle's ice-axe, and come to our help. The three of us would then rescue the others. Jungle acknowledged his instructions and told us he was setting off.

I hope I never have to endure such an ordeal again. Every minute was an hour, every hour an eternity. A hasty move on my part might send both Constant and myself crashing into the abyss. My nose itched, but I dared not scratch it; it froze, but I dared not rub it. I was getting colder and colder. Constant, with whom I could converse in shouts, was in a similar predicament. He was unhurt, but as cold and miserable as I was, if not more so.

After a long time the radio buzzed. It was Jungle. He had lost his way.

My heart sank, and Burley, who was listening in, gave a groan. It was surely all up with us now. I was suddenly seized with an overwhelming sense of the pathos of it all. We, who had set off so confidently, who had worked so hard and come so far; we who were our country's hope and a world's heroes: we were to perish miserably in this stern country, far from home and dear ones.

It was so sad that I could not hold back the tears. The tears froze immediately and I found myself stuck to the glacier by two icicles and in an even worse state than before.

I told Constant the news and did my best to comfort him. Poor fellow, he took it well, and so did Burley when I spoke to him. If we were to die, at least we would die like gentlemen.

There was still hope that Jungle would find us, but so low was I that I put little trust in him.

The day wore on.

I was, I think, half unconscious when an idea came to me. The porters! They had saved us before; could they save us again?

The only way of communicating with them was via Prone. None of the porters would touch the radio; I think they thought it was witchcraft. The question was: was Prone within hearing of a radio, was the radio operational, and was he in fit condition to answer it?

I called and waited, called and waited again; and went on calling. I became frantic with anxiety.

Then I realized that I was doing it wrong. I stopped buzzing and spoke into the microphone:

'Binder to Ailing. Binder to Ailing. Are you receiving me? Over.'

And then came the words that will ring in my ears to my dying day.

'Ailing to Binder. Ailing to Binder. Receiving you loud and clear. Are you receiving me? Over.'

I could have wept – had not the icicles been a reminder of the folly of doing so. I explained the situation to Prone and asked him to get the Bang. He did so, and I began the difficult business of instructing him. Constant translated my messages into Yogistani and I passed them on as accurately as I could to Prone, who gave them at third hand to Bing.

It was hopeless. My stomach and Prone's were quite unused to pronouncing Yogistani. The noises we produced would have been a disgrace in any company; as vehicles of communication they were a total failure. Constant said that the replies which I passed on to him bore no relation at all to the problem under consideration. They would, he said, if uttered in the streets of Chaikhosi, result in imprisonment for life, if not worse. They were, he imagined, without precedent or parallel in the whole history of spoken language.

He himself had never imagined that such statements were possible; if he ever came out of the crevasse alive he would have to reconsider his whole philosophy in the light of what I had said. He begged me to keep my stomach closed and tell Prone to do the same. If the least suspicion of what he had heard should reach the ears of the Bang, the result might well be a massacre; at the very least, the porters would desert, or would be incapacitated for further work.

This was serious. There remained one hope: was Prone fit to travel?

No, he said; it was out of the question. His legs would not support him.

But he could be carried? Yes; he was fit enough for that.

And so it was arranged. Again, we waited, but this time in high hope. Prone, carried by the Bang, gave us a running commentary on his progress.

Then they were with us: Bing, short and immensely powerful, with Prone pick-a-back; Bung, shorter still but equally sturdy; and a third porter, Bo by name, who was even shorter and sturdier.

In no time my icicles were hacked away and Constant hauled to the surface, chilled but otherwise none the worse. Bing and Bung were despatched to the rescue of the others, while Constant and I staggered back to Base Camp accompanied by Bo with Prone on his back.

The others returned within the hour. Bing had climbed up to Shute and brought him down under his arm, and later had done the same for Wish. Both were shaken by their ordeal and had to be treated with champagne. Burley, who had been carried back, went to bed with a bottle.

The question now was: where was Jungle? We called him by radio but failed to make contact. Shute said that we had probably seen the last of him; he would turn up next year in

Vladivostock, or the year after that in Valparaiso, and write a book entitled *Route-finding in Asia and America*. He said that since Jungle was aiming for Base Camp it was a mathematical certainty that he would never reach it; we had better forget about him.

I could only conclude that Shute was still suffering from shock.

A search party was clearly the thing. But none of us was fit to go out again. Could the porters help us? Constant put it to the Bang. The latter immediately called out the porters and made them form a straight line with one end at the camp and the other far out on the glacier. With the camp as centre they described a circle, and it was not long before Jungle was caught and restored to us, tired but sound. He was quite surprised to find that we had been anxious about him and inclined to take it as a reflection on his competence. I told him that he must allow for our natural over-anxiety at the bare possibility of losing him. He saw my point, and seemed satisfied.

*

Next day we held a council of war. The North Wall was proving a tougher proposition than we had anticipated; our plans would have to be drastically revised. Moreover, Burley said that he would not in any circumstances allow himself to be alone on a rope again with Wish. He had, he said, promised his fiancée that he would take no unnecessary risks, and cragsmen who became cragbound at the very earliest opportunity were clearly an unnecessary risk. He said that his frequently-expressed opinion of the nuisance value of scientists upon mountains had been fully vindicated. A mountaineer scientist was, he said, one of the worst and most dangerous types of split personality, and not to be relied upon except to do the wrong thing.

Wish retorted that the leading man on a rope had the right to expect help from the second. If Burley had been half a mountaineer, instead of wholly a handicap, yesterday's unfortunate incident would never have occurred. He said that big men were notoriously clumsy on crags, and it would suit *him* very well indeed if Burley stayed at the bottom of the mountain, where he could do the least amount of damage. Those of us who had fiancées, he said, owed it to them to keep as far away from Burley as possible.

Jungle broke in now, saying that he himself had no fiancée, but if he had he would consider it his elementary duty to keep away from Shute, who, he said, was as little to be trusted with an ice axe as a Red Indian on the warpath. Shute, considerably agitated I thought, said that *his* fiancée had expressly warned him against passengers who let other people do all the work and got lost when their turn came. He said that the sight of Jungle on the other end of one's rope was enough to make the safest iceman drop his axe. He said that nothing would induce him to venture out alone with Jungle again.

All this was somewhat bewildering. It was quite clear, of course, that my companions had not yet recovered from their recent shaking-up. That portion of their remarks which was not friendly plain speaking was doubtless due to nervous reaction from their ordeal; in a day or two they would be their normal hearty selves again. In the meantime I had the responsibility of nursing two friendships, and this did not promise to be easy. My mind was further confused by trying to decide who had a fiancée and who had not.

In the end, all I could think of was to remind them again that Rum Doodle was not Mont Blanc. Shute said that he was glad to be reminded of this, as he had completely forgotten the fact. He asked me if I could recall any of Totter's remarks on the subject which might be of help to him in future. I quoted to him Totter's famous remark: to climb Mont Blanc is one thing; to climb Rum Doodle is quite another. Shute thanked me and said that this was one of the soundest things he had ever heard; it would, he said, be a great inspiration to him. He would be quite conscious in future that he was not on Mont Blanc, and would behave accordingly. He said that had he been on Mont Blanc he would have been delighted to have Jungle as his partner; as, however, he was not on Mont Blanc, but on Rum Doodle, he insisted on having a third person on the rope – preferably a porter.

This seemed reasonable enough. Yesterday's lesson was that two on a rope were ill-fitted to cope with an emergency. A porter with each pair would greatly increase our factor of safety. But since the bivouac tents were made to accommodate two, it would have to be four on a rope: two Europeans and two porters. This arrangement would have the additional advantage that the porters would be able to carry complete equipment for all four, so that each rope would be a self-contained unit capable of looking after itself, if necessary, for several days.

Burley pointed out that this would upset all our planning; but since it would mean that he would no longer have Wish all to himself he was heartily in favour of it. The others were just as enthusiastic, and we decided to adopt the idea. I was greatly pleased by our unanimity, which seemed to me to reflect the spirit of the expedition.

7

The North Wall Conquered

On the following day we set off once more. Burley was too weak to leave his sleeping-bag so I sent Shute and Constant away together with their two porters, followed by Wish and Jungle with theirs. Before setting off myself I sent a runner with a despatch: 'Reorganizing for second assault on North Wall. All fit and well. Team spirit beyond praise and the porters are excellent.'

That day's work was truly phenomenal. On arriving at the foot of his ice slope Shute wisely decided to give his porters lessons in icecraft. He first showed them how to cut steps, then let them try it for themselves. They picked it up very quickly – so quickly, in fact, that Shute and Constant could hardly keep up with them. They mounted the steep slope as rapidly as they were able to climb in the rarefied atmosphere. Both said they had never seen anything like it. The porters showed no sign of tiring; they kept on and on, in spite of their full loads and the work of chipping steps in hard ice.

When Wish and Jungle arrived at the ice wall the first party were nearly out of sight. It would obviously have been foolish to ignore so satisfactory a staircase, and they abandoned the idea of tackling the rock-face again.

I arrived some hours later. By this time neither party was to be seen. I called Wish on the radio. He told me what had happened. He said that all the Europeans were on the verge of exhaustion due to the pace set by the porters. They would certainly reach the South Col. He advised me to go back to Base Camp and follow next day with all the equipment needed at Advanced Base. He particularly asked me not to forget the medical equipment, which was likely to be of more use there than at Lower Base.

So back I went to Base Camp, not sorry to have a chance to rest and to spend some friendly hours with Burley. My affection for this forthright giant had been growing ever since our first meeting. A leader should not have favourites, but I must confess that from all my companions I would have chosen Burley to share a tent with.

I found him in his sleeping-bag and said that I proposed to spend the night with him. He said it was kind of me, but he really thought that Prone needed me more than he did. Prone, he said, would be left quite alone at Base and would be happier during his lonely vigil if he had the memory of one night of companionship. This was very unselfish of him and, disappointed though I was, I could not but see that my duty was with the lonely one.

I found him in his sleeping bag. He also was grateful but unselfish, saying that he would not dream of depriving Burley of my company. I told him I would not hear of such a sacrifice, and soon we were settled in for the night.

Poor Prone seemed quite low, and to brighten him up I encouraged him to talk about his home. Had he a fiancée? I asked. He said no, his wife was the unsympathetic kind and his children considered one mother quite enough.

I apologized for my blunder, but said I was surprised to hear that he was married; Sir Hugeley had told me that he was a bachelor. Prone said that Sir Hugeley was welcome to his opinion on this, as on every other subject; but his own impression was different. I said that I supposed he found family life congenial. He said, on the contrary, he found it unsupportable.

He told me one day that he was being followed by a lurking suspicion. p.27

The great question was: would it go? p.33

We roped up for the first time. p.35

I must admit that I was completely baffled. p.36

Poor fellows, they were still slightly hysterical. **p.44**

had already
nnoitred
lower slopes
he wall.

Burley was completely exhausted. p.56

I could only conclude that Shute was still suffering from shock. p. 59

Burley was still sleeping-bag ridden.
But he appeared, good fellow that he is,
to see me depart. p.67

I found myself concentrating on the seat of Constant's trousers. p.83

We made no attempt this time to leave Pong behind. p.90

'I will live!' I cried, and fell flat on my face. p.123

So down I went to Advanced Base. p.129

One day later we were all together for the first time for nearly a fortnight. p.129

He went quite giddy and fell on his hip. **p.140**

I urged him to tell me more, saying that a trouble shared was a trouble halved. The poor fellow was reluctant at first, but I overcame his shyness and he told me his sad story. He was of poor family. His father was an unemployed oil-stroker of the old-fashioned sort with a strong pride in his craft and a horror of receiving charity. To send his son to medical college he forced himself to swallow his pride. Prone said that the daily sight of his father swallowing his pride had been the strongest impression of his early man-hood. Not only did his father swallow his pride, he wore it to the bone for the sake of his son, drawing benefit from six different charities under eight different names, writing beg-ging, threatening and anonymous letters, picking pockets, robbing mail-vans and women's handbags, burgling houses, taking toffee from children and writing penitent articles for revivalist journals. Such willing and grinding sacrifice had inspired the young Prone to dedicate himself to the fulfil-ment of his father's desire. He resolved that no obstacle should prevent him from attaining the distant goal of GP.

After many years of devoted study his ambition was achieved. To provide the money for his purchase of a prac-tice his father made the final sacrifice, accepting the honorary treasurership of a charitable organization which offered un-limited scope for embezzlement. Prone became a practising doctor.

His very first patient was a widow suffering from acute horror and malevolence due to reading her small son's com-ics. She hated the young doctor at first sight and made up her horrible mind to marry him. She told him that unless he took her to wife she would accuse him publicly of having mislaid her medical card. Rather than risk disgrace and the shatter-ing of his father's dreams, Prone consented. They were married at Gravesend on Hallowe'en.

His married life had been a long martyrdom. His wife, he said, was a fiend in human shape. A gracious lady to the outside world, she was a devil to him. The things she did were too horrible to be mentioned. Their children, who numbered eight and one to come, were fitting offspring of such a monster, each more loathsome than the last – the one to come being, by a process of extrapolation, truly ghastly in his imagination. Nobody, said Prone, could possibly have the faintest idea of what he had gone through. His Saturday afternoons were nightmares.

I was deeply grieved by this pathetic story. I told Prone that he had my full sympathy and offered my help in any way which might be of use to him. He said that it was very kind of me; as a matter of fact there was one little thing I could do: he wished to test an anti-pester serum; did I mind if he tried it on me?

Naturally I was glad, both at his change of mood and of my chance to be of use to him. He got out his hypodermic syringe and gave me a large injection.

He told me afterwards that he was quite satisfied with the result. The effect was to send me to sleep at once; and so ended the only heart-to-heart talk which I was able to have with Prone.

*

Next morning I rose late, feeling for some reason quite below par. I had the task of organizing the porters in Constant's absence without understanding a word of their language. Luckily, the equipment was already prepared; all I had to do was to get hold of the porters one by one and lead them to their loads. It turned out, however, that they had their own ideas as to who was to carry what, and a good deal of confusion resulted. We were just ready by lunch time, when, of course, they all went off to eat. After lunch it all had to be gone through again, and it was quite late when we were at last ready to move off.

I had difficulty in persuading Prone to allow the medical equipment out of his hands, but he finally agreed to let me take it, after taking out anything which he himself might need. We had a long discussion about whether the champagne – which, of course, was part of the medical equipment – should be taken to the South Col. We compromised by leaving one case behind; he needed it particularly, he said, as he was about to contract anaemia.

Burley was unable to give me any help, being still sleeping-bag-ridden. But he appeared, good fellow that he is, to see me depart. He was disturbed when he saw that I had the medical equipment; he had not realized that it was going to the South Col.

We set off, after I had taken an affectionate farewell of Prone, and had gone only a little way when Burley overtook us. He did not like, he said, to see me going off alone, and as he was suddenly feeling much better he had decided to accompany me. He would, he said, be able to acclimatize more quickly on the Col.

I was both impressed by his fortitude and touched by his consideration. It may have been due to his kindness that I felt homesick that morning. I told Burley about my family and friends and showed him some photographs when we halted. The dear fellow was quite gruff – one might almost have said rude. He, too, was evidently feeling the pull of home and found it difficult to hide his feelings. I put a friendly hand on his shoulder, and he gave a little snort. That snort told me more than words could have expressed. I suspected that his decision to accompany me had been wrung out of him by a desire for my companionship, and that he wished to say something to me but could not find the words.

So I said to him, kindly: 'Is there anything you want to tell me, old chap?' He said: 'Don't be a bloody fool!' which, I thought, was eloquent of the dear fellow's state of mind.

The rest of the day was a trudge up steps already cut in the steep ice. Fixed ropes had been put in the more difficult places, and we had little to do but mount steadily, maintaining the rhythm which is so necessary to high-altitude climbing. In spite of their heavy loads the porters showed no tendency to fall behind; they were doing splendidly.

In the late afternoon we strode up the last gentle slope to Advanced Base. There was no sign of life, but as we drew near the sound of loud snores from the four tents told us that our companions and their porters were recuperating after their strenuous efforts of the previous day.

We lost no time in pitching our tents, and soon Pong was busy over the pressure stoves. How he came to be at Advanced Base I was unable to decide; certainly I had had no intention of bringing him with me. I wondered, in one moment of ungallant suspicion, whether Prone had pushed him on to the end of our procession. It would have been an unBritish thing to do; but the temptation would be great, and a sick man might well be forgiven for yielding to it. I must say, in fairness to Prone, that he repudiates any such action. His theory is that Pong came along of his own initiative, being furious at the thought of losing so many victims.

Be that as it may, the others, when they emerged from their tents at the cry of 'Come and get it!' were, in their turn, furious when they recognized the familiar handiwork, and I am obliged to record that hard words were said. My plea of innocence was met by a counter-charge of incompetence, and dinner, besides being, as usual, the day's worst ordeal, was also the occasion of acrimony.

It was clear to me that we were not yet acclimatized; and this was confirmed by the others. They had, they said, been completely worn out by the hard pace set by the porters in their step cutting. They advised great caution in the employment of porters for this purpose; their brute strength and endurance was to be reckoned as one of the natural hazards of mountaineering in Yogistan.

This was a serious matter. There can be no doubt that the Yogistani is a natural mountaineer. When he becomes sufficiently civilized and educated to climb mountains voluntarily he may well be unapproachable. But so long as the initiative and the organizational responsibility rest with his Sahibs his undoubted powers must be kept under control. To reach the summit of Rum Doodle a partnership of brain and brawn was necessary; the brawn was indispensable, but it must be subordinated to the direction of the brain. We agreed that in future the porters should be restrained from endangering the health and safety of the party.

*

Before turning in that night I walked out to a small prominence above the camp to survey the view. The view was breathtaking. To the left North Doodle towered above the little camp, inhospitable and awe-inspiring. To the right the great shoulder of Rum Doodle itself soared above me, bleak and dreadful in the evening light. Below, on the glacier, Base Camp was a group of dots. The glacier wound away into the distance, losing itself among a chaos of snow-capped peaks and pinnacles. To the East a wilderness of desolation extended, peak after mighty peak, as far as the eye could see. It was breathtaking. Spires and pinnacles soared skyward in profusion, taking one's breath away.

Breathless, I returned to my tent, to find Burley already in his sleeping-bag and occupying three-quarters of the floor space. I wriggled into the remaining quarter as best I could, grateful for being no bigger than I am. Burley and I were together at last; I hoped that we would continue the confidences of the afternoon.

We lay in silence for a while, then I suggested that Burley might like to tell me about his fiancée. He said why? and I thought I detected a reticence. I said that talking about family and friends drew men closer together. He said that since I put it like that he didn't mind telling me; but it was not an easy thing to talk about and I would understand that he was not in the habit of chattering about it to any busybody.

I said, of course, I quite understood, and would value his confidence all the more on that account. He told me that he had found his fiancée one Saturday afternoon behind the sideboard in his father's dining room. She was slight and small and had a club-foot and a hare-lip and, consequently, a limp and a lisp. She was near-sighted and carried an ear-trumpet, being too nervous to use electrical equipment to aid her deafness. She was either colour-blind or had a bad memory for names. She was not very good-looking, but, as Burley said, one can't have everything. She had been study-ing the structure of the sideboard on behalf of the local antiquarian society, but had unfortunately got stuck and had been there a fortnight when Burley found her, being either too timid to call for help or too weak to make herself heard. Burley had rescued her single-handed, and this had been the turning-point of his life. He had, he said, realized at last his boyhood dream of rescuing a maiden in distress, and felt bound to fall in love with her. This he had done. She had, he said, many admirable qualities, which were none the less admirable for being hidden from the casual view. He himself was not sure what they were, which, besides giving him a sense of mystery and adventure, was proof of their delicacy. The finer qualities, he said, are never the obvious ones.

I said that I heartily agreed with him. I said also that I was touched by his story, which revealed a refinement which the unthinking would not think to find in one of his physique. I was moved to confess my affection for him and to express the hope that he and his fiancée would visit me at home.

His answer was a loud snore. Poor fellow, he must have been worn out. I made myself as comfortable as I could in my restricted space and occupied a sleepless night meditating on many things and looking forward to tomorrow's escape from Pong. Notwithstanding my discomfort it was one of the happiest nights I have ever spent. The expedition was going well; we were a united and happy party; the porters were splendid; I was with my friend. What more could a man want?

8

Advanced Base to Camp 2

The following day we regrouped. Wish had found some interesting ice which he wanted to boil, and stayed behind at Advanced Base with Burley, who was quite exhausted after his effort on the previous day and in no condition to go on. Constant and I were to escort the redundant porters back to Base Camp, returning next day. Jungle was to attempt to establish Camp 1 at 27,000 feet. Shute would follow Jungle after taking films of our various departures.

Shute had been up since dawn working on his apparatus, but it was still not operational when Jungle set off, nor an hour later when Jungle set off again, having gone round in a circle the first time. I noticed that neither of them passed any comment on the other's progress, and hoped that this was not a sign of altitude lassitude. But Jungle, when passing Shute the second time, made some remark about 'just swinging the compass', while Shute turned his handle as though taking shots. I hoped this did not indicate that they were trying to deceive each other; but I was too busy with my own affairs at the time to pay much attention. After getting ready Constant and I delayed our departure as long as we could, wishing to provide Shute with suitable material, but we were forced at last to set off unfilmed.

We reached Base Camp without incident and found Prone anaemic but cheerful. I spent the evening writing up my log and darning socks, while Constant confirmed with the porters the arrangements for moving the camp and assured me that these were thoroughly understood. It was with light hearts that we turned in for the night. Prone, with his usual unselfishness, refused to let me share his tent; he said that Constant and I, who would climb together, ought not to be parted. Constant was quite willing to let me go for one night, but I knew that Prone was right; Constant and I must lose no opportunity to learn more about each other. As it turned out, the only thing I was able to learn about Constant was that he was a good sleeper, for he dropped off as soon as I had settled down in my sleeping-bag.

We rose early, and I sent off the following despatch: 'North Wall conquered and reconnaissance of Rum Doodle begun. All well and happy and eager to come to grips with the mighty mountain which towers above us, daring us to set foot on her treacherous slopes. The team spirit remains first-rate and the porters are splendid.'

We said a final farewell to Prone. It was a deep disappointment to him – as indeed to all of us – that he was unable to accompany us; and I wondered how his father would take the news of his incapacity. To his wife, no doubt, it would provide yet another means of tormenting the poor fellow. I did my best to cheer him up. I told him that the noble way in which he had borne his sufferings was a constant example and inspiration to us all, and especially to me, who knew his sad story. He patted me on the shoulder and said: 'Yes, little man.' He seemed quite pleased.

We reached Advanced Base without incident. Constant fell into several crevasses, and myself into one or two, but we were hauled out by the porters, who were learning quickly how to use the rope. Their names were So Lo and Lo Too. They were short and sturdy. When not smoking *stunk* – which was seldom – they quarrelled, or so it appeared to me, and they took absolutely no notice of Constant and myself except when we gave them orders, which they carried out meticulously but without the least sign of interest. Constant said that since we were now above the 20,000-feet line their dispositions would improve rapidly. I watched carefully for any sign of this happening, for, to tell the truth, I was somewhat overawed by their independence and impenetrability. I knew that the East is inscrutable, but I had hardly expected it to be inscrutable to my face.

We had reached a point some little distance up the first wall of ice, climbing by the steps we had used before, when Constant drew my attention to a small figure which was approaching us from the direction of Base Camp.

There are occasions when life hits a man so hard that he feels incapable of controlling his own destiny; he is like an insect crushed beneath the foot of a giant.

This was such an occasion for me, and I could see from Constant's face that he was equally stricken.

I dropped my eyes, hoping to forget what I had seen in his.

'Can nothing be done?' I whispered.

He shook his head. 'I'll try; but it's practically hopeless.'

The small figure was climbing the steps. It was bowed almost double beneath an immense pile of kitchen utensils which clanked and rattled at every step. It ascended towards us like a figure from the nether regions, stopping finally a few yards below and turning towards us a flat nightmare of a face.

Constant engaged it in a long and violent conversation, during which So Lo and Lo Too puffed away contentedly at their pipes, while I tried to regain control of my destiny by meditating on Totter's *Thoughts at High Altitudes.*

The wrangle came to an end at last, and Constant told me that he had been quite unable to persuade Pong to return;

bribery, threats and deceit had all proved useless. Pong, he said, was evidently a man with a Purpose; short of throwing rocks at him, Constant could think of no possible way of turning him back. He had, however, told him that he should go no further than Advanced Base, where he would be needed to minister to anybody who might return from the mountain weak and helpless.

I said that this was rather hard on the weak and helpless. Constant agreed, but said he saw no alternative.

I thought for a while. The presence of Pong might endanger the whole expedition. Stomachs are delicate above 20,000 feet; specially attractive food had been incorporated in the high-altitude rations to tempt them. If Pong were to be let loose on the mountain health and hope might vanish. Was it not, perhaps, for Constant and myself to make the supreme sacrifice: to return to Base with Pong and suffer his ministrations in order to spare the rest of the team?

It was a great deal to ask of oneself. In the end I decided against it. We were needed on the mountain; we could not leave the others unsupported.

I slipped a dyspepsia tablet into my mouth and gave the word to advance.

We reached Advanced Base safely. It was deserted. I buzzed the walkie-talkie and made contact with Wish. Everybody was at Camp 1. They would spend a day or two there to acclimatize before pushing on to Camp 2.

This was satisfactory news. I told him to expect Constant and myself tomorrow and got him to describe the route. While he was speaking I distinctly heard the strains of 'Oh, My Darling Clementine' being sung in the background, and I wished myself with the happy party.

I noticed afterwards that the medical supplies were missing and surmised that they had been taken to Camp 1. This puzzled me at the time. I gathered later that it had happened by mistake.

Our meal that evening was hardly as unsavoury as I had feared it would be, being merely indigestible. But Constant said that this was probably because Pong was not yet used to high-altitude rations; in his opinion the worst was yet to come. As it was, we were both unable to sleep, and I took the opportunity to make a few kindly enquiries about Constant's private life. I told him that it was not quite clear to me which of our party had fiancées and which had not, and I asked him if he had one. He said no. I asked him if his parents were still living. He said yes. I asked him if he had any brothers and sisters. He said yes. I told him I had three sisters. He said Oh.

There was something wrong here; nobody with a sense of atmosphere could be unaware of it. I lay for a while wondering how I might make contact with him and thinking how lonely is the human spirit, especially in grief. I suspected that Constant's taciturnity hid an aching heart.

This is the sort of situation which a conscientious leader often meets and is possibly the one case when it is kinder to ignore the other's feelings. Although it is difficult to speak of one's troubles it is always a relief; it is generally a greater kindness to make a sufferer speak of his sufferings than to respect his superficial desire to suffer them in silence.

The best way to invite a confidence is to give one. Guessing that Constant's reluctance was associated with an unhappy love affair I related to him an experience of my own which, although it caused me pain at the time, was now over and done with. I hoped that this would encourage him with the hope that his pain, too, would pass.

He made no comment on my story, so I remarked that such things happened to most of us.

Again, there was no reply. But I became aware of a peculiar sound, and on looking at Constant I saw that he was curled up in his sleeping bag, quivering.

The poor fellow was sobbing!

Deeply moved, I put my hand on his shoulder. The sobbing became more violent.

'Tell me about it, old chap,' I said.

I thought he was going to lose control of himself altogether. But gradually the paroxysm passed. He turned over, and I saw that his cheeks were wet with tears.

'Tell me,' I said again.

He hastily covered his face as a few last sobs were wrenched from him. Then he lay quite still.

I could not help being aware that the atmosphere had changed, and I waited now in anticipation. I was not disappointed. He began to speak, slowly at first, hesitatingly; then with increasing fluency.

As a boy Constant had been a circus addict, and his passion, though discouraged by his parents, had continued throughout his life, changing only to mature with increasing age. His happiest memories were all connected with the circus; its peculiar blending of personality, grandiloquence and fantasy appealed to some deeply rooted romantic hunger. It was, he said, the same urge which dictated his choice of career. The people of the circus were to him more than ordinary people; they were at once his knights in armour, his fairies, his gnomes, his childhood princes and princesses. All his childish romances centred on the circus.

And his first and only love had been a circus artiste.

Her name was Stella. She performed with a troupe of seals. She was, said Constant, the loveliest creature in the world. Noblemen and princes worshipped her; but she was a simple girl at heart and would have none of them; she had vowed to marry a simple man and bear him simple children.

They loved at first sight and were happy as only first lovers can be. He saw her every performance; she kissed her hand to him twice nightly with matinées on Wednesdays and Saturdays.

There was but one flaw in the perfection of their private heaven. Travers, the chief male seal, took a dislike to Constant. Stella said it was jealousy. He barked whenever Constant approached her, and during performances he would come to the edge of the ring and pull faces at him, frightening the children. He began to refuse his food. The climax came when Stella walked on wearing Constant's engagement ring for the first time. When he saw it Travers uttered a cry which tore the hearts of all present. He flung himself on the ground and buried his face in his flippers.

Stella was heartbroken. She was greatly attached to her seals and felt their troubles as if they had been her children. She told Constant that she could not bear to hurt Travers any longer. She had, moreover, great faith in his judgment; his aversion to Constant might indicate some serious defect in character which was hidden to her. Unless he could make friends with the animal it must be all over between them.

Constant vowed he would do it. It was an adventure after his own romantic heart. He sent to all corners of the sea for fishy delicacies and spent all his leisure at Travers' tank, tempting him. But the poor animal remained unmoved. He would eat only from Stella's hand, and little enough at that. He became as thin as an eel.

Constant was frantic. He consulted authorities on seal psychology and visited ancient seamen in various hemispheres. He sat for hours in his bath trying to put himself in Travers' place. His toes became permanently wrinkled, but the secret of the seal's affection remained hidden from him.

One day, while strolling in the blackest despair through the West End of London, little caring what happened to him, he was seized by an uncontrollable impulse to justify his misery by performing some irretrievable act of degradation. Uttering a cry which changed the lives of three bystanders, he flung himself madly into a news cinema. A cartoon was just beginning. It opened with a rocky shore where a pretty mermaid was charming the creatures of the deep with a song. Amongst her audience was a large, healthy-looking seal which was listening with an expression of complete ecstasy. With a thrill, Constant saw that it was the image of Travers in his happier moments.

He dashed from the cinema and took a taxi straight to the circus, where he rushed to Travers' tank and laid bare his soul in a passionate rendering of 'Caller Herrin''.

The effect was startling. Lions roared, dogs howled, elephants trumpeted and stamped. An acrobat fell on his friend and three clowns gave their notice on the spot.

But Constant was oblivious to these trivia. For Travers was sitting up in the water with a smile of ultimate bliss, accompanying Constant in a well-modulated bass voice.

The circus manager rushed in and offered Constant a contract at a fabulous salary. Constant brushed him aside and hurried to Stella's dressing-room. Back they came together, and Constant and Travers continued their duet.

Stella gave a cry of love and flung herself at the ecstatic Constant. As she did so Travers gave a thunderous bellow. Astonished, she turned to the beast and tried to stroke its head. To her horror it bit her hand.

That was the end. The animal had transferred its affections to Constant and was insanely jealous of Stella. Heartbroken and furious, she told him to take the beast he had stolen and go. He clasped Travers in his arms and ran sobbing into the street, where he took a taxi to the zoo. All the time, Travers had continued to render his part of 'Caller Herrin''.

Constant was sobbing again, his face hidden in his sleeping-bag. I waited until the fit had passed, then assured him of my deepest sympathy and said that I knew what a relief it must have been to tell me about it. He nodded. He was, he said, feeling better already. He had even begun to hope that he had at last conquered his grief.

I turned from him to wipe away a tear. The rewards of leadership are not always so immediate or so intense. When I had composed myself I asked him what had happened to Travers. The animal, he told me, had started a male voice choir among the zoo seals. Constant sang with them on Saturday afternoons.

*

That night both Constant and I slept badly. I had a recurring nightmare in which I saw Constant's face at the moment when he recognized Pong as the figure following us. But when it came closer it turned out to be a flat-faced seal which sobbed heartbrokenly and tried to hide itself in a sleeping-bag which was much too small for it. I awoke unrested. Constant was also tired out, having been seized with repeated bouts of sobbing which made the tent shake. He said they were due to habit and did not indicate grief any more, which was a comfort to me.

We were really in no condition to go on, but the mountain was less terrifying than the prospect of Pong's meals. We left him behind with great relief and assurances that we had never eaten so well in our lives. We told him that we would hurry back to partake as soon as possible of his culinary marvels. This, we assured him, would be the high spot of our adventure, the reward for difficulties surmounted, the silver lining to our cloud of toil. We begged him to stay where he was so as not to disappoint us.

We left him washing up and glowering.

We set off for Camp 1 by the route which Wish had described to us. Just above the Advanced Base a steep ridge rose for some five thousand feet before merging into the face of the mountain. Our path lay up the left face of this ridge.

Constant and I were using oxygen. We found the apparatus so uncomfortable that we allowed So Lo to lead. The porters refused the aid of oxygen; I think they thought it was witchcraft.

After a short distance the ground steepened, and soon we – or rather the porters – were cutting steps in hard ice. We were now high. Every step climbed demanded an effort equivalent to running up 153 steps at sea level – the figure is Wish's. The great ordeal had begun at last. We could now number ourselves amongst those who had trod the ultimate heights and invaded nature's last stronghold against the advancing spirit of man.

I tried to remember all I had read about climbing at such heights. I took one step, then waited for ten minutes. This, I understood, was essential; our predecessors were unanimous about it: one step, then ten minutes rest, or seven in an emergency. I found it more difficult than I had anticipated. To remain in one position for ten minutes was not at all easy. First, I tended to fall over sideways; then I got cramp in the calf; then my nose started to itch; then my foot started to vibrate and had to be held down by both hands. This was very tiring, and when I crouched to hold my foot I was lower than I had been before making the step, which caused me to wonder whether I was gaining height or losing it; and the mental strain was so great that I lost control of myself and fell off my step.

I was pulled up by So Lo, and tried again. I was beginning to appreciate all I had read concerning the rigours of high altitude climbing. But I noticed that the others seemed to be ignoring the procedure. While I was struggling to maintain my posture they would shuffle about freely on their steps and even show signs of impatience. This I could understand in the case of the porters; but Constant, I thought, should know better. I was about to expostulate when he said: 'What on earth do you think you're doing, Binder?' I explained, and to my surprise he went off into fits of laughter. He said that the early climbers had been forced to rest after every few steps because they were out of breath. This was because they were not using oxygen. Nobody, he said, need rest any longer than he wanted to; at my rate of progress we should never get up the mountain.

This was a surprise to me, but after thinking it over it seemed quite reasonable, and I decided to give it a fair trial. I found to my delight that the going was not appreciably heavier than it had been the previous day. I mention this incident, in which I appear in no very admirable light, because it is a striking illustration of how one may be misled by book knowledge. It was a lesson to me, as a reader, to take nothing on trust, and as a writer to take the greatest care not to mislead my readers.

I hate to think what my progress might have been, had Constant not been there to put me right.

I soon found the going quite difficult enough, and I began to expect the onset of those strange phenomena which occur in rarefied atmospheres. I reminded Constant that I would like to hear of any unusual experiences he might have, and when we stopped for a rest I called the others on the radio and reminded them of the same thing. They were still at Camp 1, not yet acclimatized. Burley, to whom I spoke, told me that Wish was being particularly objectionable that morning; did I think this was one of the symptoms I was interested in? I assured him that it undoubtedly was, and thanked him. Wish apparently seized the apparatus at this point, for his voice now came through telling me that there was every reason for his attitude. Burley had snored heavily the whole night and Wish had been quite unable to get a wink. The snores, he said, were not, as he had expected, attenuated due to the rarefied atmosphere, but were much louder, more complicated and altogether more objectionable than they had ever been before. This, he said, was an example of how a man's true and bestial nature is revealed at high altitudes. Burley was clearly unfitted for social life above 20,000 feet – if, indeed, he could be considered fit for it at any altitude.

I commiserated with Wish, but asked him to be kind to his friend, who had much to bear. He promised to remember my words and asked me to keep a look-out for Wharton's warples.

Off we went again, climbing well, restraining the impetuous So Lo, who was inclined to rush the mountain – a fault to which all beginners are prone. A novice will tire himself out within an hour while the veteran keeps going all day at the same steady pace.

Higher and higher we climbed, and all the time our legs grew weaker and our breathing more laboured. It was now becoming necessary to stop quite often, but at first I found it almost a pleasure to stop because I had to and not because I *thought* I had to. The magnificent scenery around me had become much less interesting. I found myself concentrating on the seat of Constant's trousers – he being ahead of me. I thought I had never seen such a disgusting trousers' seat in all my life. I thought that Constant ought to be ashamed of himself for owning such a seat. I thought how different was the seat of Burley's trousers. I noted this down in my diary that evening as an interesting effect of high altitude.

We reached 27,000 feet in remarkably good time, and looked around for Camp 1. To our dismay it was nowhere to be seen. I called up the others on the radio. Shute answered. I described to him as well as I could the route we had taken and the nature of our immediate surroundings. He said that as far as he could make out we were actually at Camp 1. He advised me to find some high spot from which we might get a good view. This was all very well, but the face of the ridge at this point was a maze of high spots; the tents might be hidden behind any one of a hundred crags or pinnacles. We reconnoitred and we shouted. We whistled and we yodelled. We exploded paper bags. All to no result.

We had just sat down to think it over when Constant gave a strangled cry and pointed downward.

Below, ascending by the steps we had cut, was a dark and grim figure.

Pong!

This was awful.

We held a hurried council of war. Pong was heavily laden. He seemed to have brought all the cooking equipment and most of the food we had left at Advanced Base. It was just possible that we could shake him off. We would abandon the search for Camp 1. We would climb as quickly and as high as we could and establish Camp 2 when we could go no further.

While we were talking Pong had drawn alarmingly close, and when we moved off I had to fight against unmanly panic. Constant said he had known nothing like it since being chased by a bull at Broadstairs on bank holiday.

We gave So Lo his head with the step-cutting and did our

best to keep up with him. He set a tremendous pace. I doubt whether steps have ever been cut so quickly at any altitude. There was something unnatural about it. Mountaineering at 27,000 feet was supposed to be something almost super-human; yet So Lo, without oxygen, was cutting steps as quickly as we, with oxygen, could climb them. It was all wrong; and it worried me. I was also worried about Constant's bull. It seemed to me very unlikely that there should be a loose bull at Broadstairs on bank holiday. Was Constant deceiving me? I also felt ashamed of myself for doubting him, which added to my worries.

In spite of our spanking pace Pong continued to gain on us. Faster and faster we went. Constant and I became dizzy and fell frequently. I became a mass of bruises, and Constant was in even worse condition; being taller than I he had further to fall. The climax came when, after a particularly bad fall, he found himself being picked up by Pong, who had caught us up. Constant uttered a horrid cry and collapsed, senseless. I revived him by hitting his head, and asked him what we should do. He said that since I was obviously in no condition to go on we had better camp where we were. This we did. I found that the height was 29,000 feet. We had established Camp 2 as originally planned. But this was small satisfaction to us at the time; we could think of nothing but the digestive horrors to come.

9

The Missing Camp

Sometimes, even now, I awake in the night screaming as I relive in dreams the misery of that wretched night. As soon as the tents were up Constant and I crept into our sleeping-bags and awaited supper. I prepared myself for the ordeal by thinking about Christian martyrs and reminding myself that Rum Doodle would hardly be worth climbing if it were no more than a pleasure trip. But my meditations were interrupted by a prolonged clattering which came from the direction of Pong's tent. Constant, whose nerve was beginning to go, went out to investigate. He came back trembling, with an ominous tale. Pong was crouched over a large stewpan, from which emerged indescribable odours. The ground in front of the tent was littered with empty food tins, and Constant had ascertained that their contents had been those special delicacies which we had chosen to attract the high altitude palate. And when it appeared, the loathsome mess confirmed his forebodings. All our choicest titbits had gone into Pong's awful pot: our luscious breast of chicken, the tinned apricots and cream which we had so often tasted in anticipation, the sardines, the caviar, the lobster, the lovely gruyère cheese, the pickled walnuts, the curry, the salmon, even the coffee and the chocolate biscuits: all these were reduced to a nauseating brew which might have sent Macbeth's witches shrieking from the place.

The horrors of that meal were but the prelude to a night such as few human beings can have endured. It was, I think, about midnight when I awoke from a nightmare in which I was buried under Rum Doodle, to find Constant lying across my chest snoring heavily and muttering. When I pushed him off he awoke with a cry of terror and hit me on the nose, making my eyes water. I apologized for waking him, and we settled down again. I must have dozed off, for I awoke suddenly under the impression that a prehistoric monster had crept into the tent and was about to do me an injury. I seized the nearest solid object – which happened to be a climbing boot – and hit the monster as hard as I could. It was Constant, of course. I asked had I woken him; and if he said what I thought he said he is not the man I think he is. I decided after careful thought that I must have imagined it, and was just dropping off again when Constant uttered a wild cry and bit me in the ear. I woke him up and suggested that it might be safer to sleep head to foot. After some strange remarks he agreed, and I started to shuffle around in my sleeping-bag. It was breathless work at that altitude. I had to stop three times to rest, and when I finally completed the turn I found that I had lost my pillow on the way. I could not face the thought of searching for it, so I made a boot do instead.

I was almost asleep again when a horrid noise sounded a few inches from my face. Terrified, I struck out instinctively, and found myself grasping, of all things, a mouth. This was quite horrible; I don't think I shall ever forget the alarm and disgust which it caused me. We found out later that we had both turned round together and were still sleeping head to head. Waking suddenly out of the nightmare caused by the clutch on his mouth, Constant flung himself upon me. Still dazed by sleep and terror I fought back madly, and we were wrestling all over the tent. I was soon exhausted, and had almost given up hope of surviving when Constant stopped suddenly and lay where he was, panting. When we had recovered our breath and wits I apologized again, and we tried to disentangle ourselves. But this was not as easy as one might expect. We were locked in a complicated embrace, half in and half out of our sleeping-bags, with ropes and clothing wrapped around us. It was pitch dark. In the middle of the operation I dropped off to sleep in a sitting position, to wake screaming under the impression that the rope was a snake which was trying to strangle me. I struggled desperately with the rope before I came to my senses, making the tangle ten times worse.

We went to it again, but somehow we could never make each other understand what we were trying to do. Sometimes we would be pulling in opposite directions on the same section of rope; sometimes we would roll over and get our legs entangled; sometimes we would strike out in a bold bid to free an arm, and catch each other in the eye. We were continually out of breath. Every other minute one of us would be seized with cramp or stomach-ache and writhe about, making it all worse than ever. We kept falling asleep and waking terrified after the most hideous nightmares.

Finally, the tent came down on us.

After that we gave it up. We just stayed where we were and waited for daylight.

When it was light enough to see we got our heads out somehow and looked at each other.

'This can't go on,' said Constant.

This, I thought, was very well put. At all costs we must get down to Camp 1.

But first we had to get out of the tent, which was no light matter at 29,000 feet. After a few moments of struggle we were forced to stop to regain our breath. Our hands were freezing; we had to put on gloves, which made the job of disentangling almost impossible. At one point I almost gave up in despair. I lay gasping, with Constant sitting on my head, my arms bound behind me with rope, my legs wrapped in tent and sleeping-bag. For the third time I faced the possibility of defeat. Was the mountain too strong for us, after all?

To make matters worse, Pong came with breakfast.

After a sharp and manly struggle with nausea, Constant sent Pong for So Lo and Lo Too. Soon they were working on us, and at last, after what seemed an eternity, we were free men.

Telling the porters to re-erect the tent we retired to theirs, where we spent some time boiling our boots in order to de-ice them. Pong followed us with breakfast, which was a rehash of yesterday's left-overs made still more deplorable by burning. We forced ourselves to swallow a few mouthfuls, holding our noses and closing our eyes and telling ourselves that it was for the sake of the expedition. Then we took some stomach tablets and made our plans. They were simple. We must make Camp 1 as quickly as possible and spread the burden of Pong as widely as we could.

We radioed the others and told them to expect us; but we said nothing about Pong, not daring to risk a panic on the mountain. Jungle told me that they would wait for us. Burley, he said, had just become acclimatized but thought that a further day at Camp 1 would consolidate his fitness. The others, too, thought they would benefit from an extra day of rest.

We moved off early. Our wet boots froze immediately; short of a rise in temperature, nothing but an amputation could have separated us from them. We fell all over the place and sometimes went to sleep where we lay. So Lo and Lo Too kept saving our lives; but at last they seemed to get tired of it, for they threw us on top of their loads and carried us for the rest of the day.

At 27,000 feet we cast about once more for Camp 1, and again, in spite of radioed instructions, we failed to find it. In desperation we decided to make for Advanced Base. We reached it in the late afternoon as exhausted as two men could possibly be.

Our first job was to thaw off our boots. This we did by putting our feet in a bucket of melted snow which we then boiled over a pressure stove. Luckily, spare boots were available. We then put a short call through to Camp 1 and went straight to bed, refusing food and drink.

*

Next day we were somewhat recovered. Under normal circumstances we should have taken a long rest, but since this would mean remaining at Pong's mercy it was not to be thought of. During the night we had crept into the mess tent and snatched a little food. Fortified by this we were able to deny ourselves breakfast, and we set off for Camp 1 shortly after sunrise. We made no attempt this time to leave Pong behind. He had by now demoralized us completely; even to refuse a meal was an act requiring the combined moral courage of both of us.

We had been somewhat cheered to learn that Shute, Jungle and Wish had already started for Camp 2. Burley, now alone at Camp 1, had unfortunately passed the peak of his acclimatization and had deteriorated during the previous day. He thought it advisable to stay behind and recuperate.

The day's climb was strenuous but uneventful. Neither Constant nor myself was fit for anything but a dogged trudge behind the porters. Ever since we had been above 20,000 feet I had been expecting the improvement in their disposition which Constant had promised. It never came. To the end they remained obedient and hard-working but completely independent and unapproachable. Constant said he could not understand this, but thought that perhaps they were not Yogistanis at all, but Rudistanis, who were a different kind of people altogether. He said he would look it up in his correspondence-course notes when he got back home.

At 27,000 feet we made our usual search, with the usual result. To this day I am utterly unable to account for our repeated failure to locate Camp 1.

Tired though we were, we had no alternative but to make for Camp 2. It was a pity to leave Burley alone at Camp 1, but I consoled myself with the thought that there would now be five of us to share the burden of Pong. Our combined wits might devise some method of circumventing him.

So it was onwards and upwards again. Using the steps we had cut two days before we mounted quickly, and Camp 2 was reached without further incident.

*

Constant and I had been miserable for so long that it was almost with surprise that we found happy people at Camp 2. As we drew near, the strains of 'Roll Out the Barrel' charmed us like the Hosannas of the Blessed.

We were welcomed with open arms and hearty back-slappings. We were punched and thumped. Our hair was ruffled. We were tripped and sat upon. Snow was put down our necks. Our bootlaces were tied together so that we fell flat on our faces.

I had not seen my comrades so boisterous since the crevasse incident. I wondered what the cause might be.

And then they saw Pong.

I have never seen a mood change so suddenly. The heaviest depression descended upon us like a plague of Egypt. The three who, one short moment before, had been as gay as sandboys, shrank into melancholy like old men. They glowered at each other and snarled maledictions. They wrung their hands and shook their heads continually. They muttered. They slunk into their tents and cowered in the corners, biting their nails and drooling. They cried quietly when no one was looking.

Coming on top of my long ordeal it was too much for me. I crept supperless into my sleeping-bag and sobbed myself to sleep.

*

I awoke next morning to find Constant sitting up in his sleeping-bag. His face was drawn.

'They've gone!' he said.

'You mean?' I gasped.

He nodded.

'Tell me,' I pleaded.

His whole frame quivered with a deep, searing sigh. His mouth opened and a long moan was forced through a tortured throat as he strained to tell the horror of it.

'Betrayed!' he groaned.

'You mean?' I said.

He nodded.

It was awful.

Gradually, I soothed him; and as the friendly sun mounted in the heavens, warming our little tent, he gathered courage. Once, when the shadow of the prowling Pong fell across the tent roof, he screamed; but soon manhood reasserted itself and he was telling me his story in a voice whose gentleness was infinitely poignant.

Jungle and Wish had crept away before dawn and fled up the mountain. Shute had left soon afterwards on his way back to Camp 1.

*

For the whole of that day we lay in our sleeping-bags, each facing the crisis in his own way. Towards evening, Constant spoke.' Tomorrow,' he said, 'I go down to Camp 1.'

I nodded. It was inevitable. I turned over and slept.

Next morning I awoke to find him gone. I was not surprised. I was not disappointed. I was hardly even interested. This was the end: the end of high endeavour, the end of comradeship, the end of dreams, the end of life itself. I stood on the brink of an infinite nothingness. Without a sigh, without a backward glance, resignedly, even thankfully, I stepped over the threshold.

*

Somebody was slapping my face in a most unpleasant manner. An impatient voice was saying: 'Wake up, Binder, you silly fool!'

I woke, opened my eyes, and looked around me.

I was lying on my back on the snow, in full and blinding daylight. Shute was bending over me.

'Where am I?' I said.

'Where do you think you are?' he asked.

I considered this for a while.

'I thought I might be in heaven,' I said.

He roared with laughter. 'I say, chaps: Binder thinks he's in heaven!'

More laughter. I looked around. Wish was there, and Jungle; and, seated on a box beside me, looking very weary, Constant.

And behind them, peering down at me, were several porters, including So Lo, Lo Too and Pong.

Then I saw the tents and began to get my bearings. It was Camp 2. Constant and I had just arrived from Advanced Base for the second time, finding the others in possession. I must have fallen asleep. The rest had been a dream.

10

Higher than Everest

After a meal which is better left undescribed we crowded into one small tent to discuss future plans. The question was: what were we to do about Pong? Several suggestions were made, but none was both practical and humane. Wish summed up in his precise way, saying that we must accept Pong as one of the hazards of the mountain and make our plans accordingly.

Constant said that he and I had had Pong for four days and it was somebody else's turn. Wish said that, in principle, he was entirely in agreement with this, but we must see how it worked out in practice. We must, he said, assume that when we split up, Pong would attach himself to the larger party in order to do the maximum amount of damage. But he could be thwarted in this by a simple stratagem. We were now five. In the morning, two would move off together to establish Camp 3, leaving three at Camp 2. Pong would naturally stay with these three. But shortly afterwards one of the three would leave, either for Camp 3 or to return to Camp 1. Again, Pong would stay with the majority. Later on, the remaining two would split, so that Pong's sphere of influence would be reduced to one.

'Isn't that rather hard on the last man?' I asked.

'It's only for a short while,' Wish assured me. 'We can change round later to suit circumstances. Is it agreed, then?'

Constant and I glanced at each other doubtfully. But Shute and Jungle said that it was a perfect scheme, and congratulated Wish on his masterly command of strategy.

'Very well,' he said. 'Now, it's obvious that Binder and Applecart are in no condition to go up to Camp 3.'

'Agreed,' said Shute and Jungle.

'In fact,' Wish continued, 'it is essential that they take a day's rest.'

'Absolutely,' said Shute and Jungle.

'So they must stay here with Pong.'

'Nothing else will do,' said Shute and Jungle.

'And now for the others,' said Wish. 'I take it that you two don't want to go together?'

'Certainly not,' said Shute and Jungle. I wondered why.

'So I shall go to Camp 3 with one of you. Which is it to be?'

'Jungle,' said Shute.

'Shute,' said Jungle.

'You'd better toss for it,' Wish suggested.

'Heads,' said Shute.

'It's tails,' said Jungle.

'Congratulations, old boy,' said Shute. 'You'll be the first to go higher than Everest.'

'But I won,' said Jungle.

'Well of course you did. The loser stays behind.'

'But I thought it was the other way round.'

'Why ever should it be?' said Shute.

'Well . . .' said Jungle.

'Of course,' Shute went on, 'if you think I'm trying to diddle you . . .'

Jungle said nothing.

'You don't trust me.'

Jungle hung his head.

'After all I've done for you.'

Jungle wriggled.

'Very well,' said Shute. 'We'll toss up again. Heads.'

'Heads it is,' said Jungle.

'My choice,' said Shute. 'I didn't like to mention it before, but I'm not feeling quite up to the mark. I daren't risk letting the side down. I will go back to Camp 1.'

Jungle looked a little bewildered. He withdrew from the conversation and sat for quite a long time with puckered brow, muttering to himself and counting off points on his fingers. From time to time he would open his mouth to speak, then think better of it. Finally, he gave a deep sigh and became quite still, staring at nothing like one who had given up all hope and was quietly waiting for death. I scented undercurrents, but I was too tired to investigate. Besides, I had other worries: how were Constant and I to endure another day at the mercy of Pong?

I put the problem to Wish, and that master-strategist produced a workable plan. Someone must decoy Pong out of the cooking tent so that someone else could steal some food, which would be concealed in the sleeping-bags of Constant and myself. Tomorrow we would live on this store, telling Pong we required no meals. We would thus have a whole day to recover our digestion. Wish suggested that those travelling with Pong should take only the plainest food, upon which his black art would have the least effect.

This was agreed upon. It was hard to forgo the dainties which we had looked forward to for so long, but it was better than having them reduced to the sickening messes which Constant and I had already endured.

The raid on the larder was organized. Jungle was sent outside to hide behind a cliff; then Constant called Pong into our tent and engaged him in conversation. They had exchanged only a few gurgles when Pong moved his head as though listening to a faint sound. The next moment he rushed from the tent and we heard him bellowing as he ran towards his kitchen.

We all hurried outside, to see Jungle flying down the mountain with Pong after him.

Wish, quick-witted as ever, dashed into the kitchen and emerged with an armful of food of various kinds. He ran straight to our tent with it; and it was lucky he did so, for Pong abandoned the chase suddenly and hurried back to the kitchen, where he squatted in the doorway glowering at us.

Jungle was now out of sight, and the general opinion was that we should never see him again. There was nothing else for it: a search-party must be organized. The porters were sent after him, while the rest of us stood by ready to defend him, with our lives if need be, against another attack.

It was two hours before the search-party returned, Jungle being carried on the back of a small but sturdy porter. Pong made no move, and we went back to our tent in peace.

Tired though I was I considered it my duty to acquaint myself with everything that had transpired since our last meeting at Advanced Base five days before. In his two days at Camp 1, Wish had melted thirteen hundredweight of ice and recalibrated his thermometers. Shute had run off two thousand feet of film and, had the lid not been accidentally knocked off his dark box, exposing the contents to daylight, some very fine sequences would have resulted. Jungle had swung his compasses higher than compasses had ever been swung before; those which survived were to be considered accurate within certain limits which he was unable to determine.

We called Burley on the walkie-talkie and learned that he was still recuperating and did not consider it advisable to move from Camp 1 just yet.

Finally, I asked if anybody had any unusual experiences to

report. The response was most interesting. Both Wish and Shute had experienced high altitude hallucinations. Wish had seen differential equations, test-tubes and Wimshurst machines, while Shute had been frightened by a vision of a camera obscura. Jungle had shown a tendency to wander when not roped to the others. He had also become convinced that he was being followed by a Prude. When asked what a Prude was he became confused. Wish said: 'Nice going, Wanderer,' as if Jungle were somehow responsible for the Prude, and they all burst out laughing. I must say the point, if any, of the joke escaped me; I daresay they were suffering from altitude hysteria.

We turned in a happy and united party, and in spite of Pong's supper I spent a reasonably comfortable night.

*

Next morning we were astir early. Jungle and Wish went off without breakfast, intending to stop for a meal as soon as they were out of sight of Pong. They took with them all the tasty food, leaving us only lentils and pemmican, which were considered to be the most Pong-proof of our supplies, being naturally unappetizing. Shute departed shortly afterwards with his one porter, leaving Constant and me with So Lo, Lo Too and Pong. We went back to our sleeping-bags, where we stayed all day, feeding ourselves on cold food and hiding the debris. In the early evening we had a call from Shute, who was safely back at Camp 1 with Burley. Burley, he said, had fully recuperated and considered himself re-climatized. He had, however, contracted sleeping-bag lassitude and did not feel justified in setting out just yet.

Wish called shortly afterwards. He and Jungle had had a hard day, but they had reached the point where the ridge on which we were climbing merged with the face of the mountain, and had established Camp 3 at 31,000 feet. Fixed ropes had been left in the difficult places. He had seen some more differential equations and two filter funnels and heard three retorts. Jungle had shown a tendency to walk backwards.

*

We rose betimes the following morning. Our private store of food had given out and we were forced to breakfast on lentils and pemmican prepared by Pong. Constant took one mouthful and turned pale. 'I'm sorry, old boy,' he said. 'I just can't face it. I must go down to Camp 1.'

This was sad news, but hardly surprising. We parted regretfully; we had been through much together. I told Constant that the manly way in which he had borne his sufferings had been a continual inspiration to me, and that I would treasure the memory of the six days we had spent together. Constant said that he, too, would not forget in a hurry.

Constant took Lo Too, leaving me So Lo and Pong. I let So Lo take the lead, wishing to conserve my mental energies. I was on the look-out for altitude hallucinations and warples. Several times I thought I saw a warple, but it turned out to be a hallucination. Several times I thought I saw a hallucination, but it turned out to be a spot on my goggles. Once I thought I saw a spot on my goggles, but it turned out to be a warple which turned out to be a hallucination. To keep my stomach-ache under control I had taken little breakfast, and was weak with hunger. I fed myself with dyspepsia tablets, which gave me a headache. I found by accident that licking the glacier-cream off my face gave my stomach some relief. Unfortunately, this resulted in both sunburn and a frozen tongue, and when I put my tongue back in my mouth to thaw it gave me toothache. I was also worried because most of my dream had come true. My four companions had dispersed exactly as they had done in the dream, which seemed sinister.

All this interfered with the rhythm which is so essential to climbing at high altitudes. I decided to forget everything else and concentrate on the rhythm. I devised a little rhyme to keep step with my feet:

> *Organ grinders, kings and queens*
> *Call for Binder's Butter Beans.*
> *Three times daily, knave and noodle*
> *Eat them gaily on Rum Doodle.**

This went round and round in my brain all day, and made such a nuisance of itself that it only added to my worries. I began to fear that I was about to lose control of my destiny.

Luckily, we reached Camp 3 before this happened. Still in control of my destiny, I greeted Wish and Jungle, who were having a rest day. In anticipation of meeting Pong again they had already dined, and they managed to keep their stores out of his reach. I dined alone on lentils and pemmican.

I was tired out, but happy in the thought that I should soon be relieved of Pong. But somehow it turned out quite differently.   Using the anti-Pong strategy which, Wish said, had worked so well at Camp 2, Wish decided that one of us must go off alone in the morning, leaving Pong with the majority of two. Later, one of these would go, leaving Pong with the last man. Since I needed a rest, I must be that last man.

Wish was very nice about it. He said I had his deepest sympathy. He said that, if anything, he was more upset about it than I was. He said that only the strictest sense of duty restrained him from insisting on taking Pong himself, whatever I might say. He said that he had never felt so acutely the conflict between personal desire and the welfare of the expedition. He said that I would understand.

I said I did indeed, and felt his distress as deeply as he did

---

* This was not true.

himself. I begged him to put a brave face on it and let duty be its own reward. He thanked me and said that he would not forget my words. It was with a sense of deep humility that I wished him good-night and went to my lonely tent.

*

And so, next morning, Wish started first, taking one porter, on an attempt to establish Camp 4. Jungle said he had deteriorated badly and must at all costs do down to Camp 1 to recuperate. While he was waiting for the day to warm up I tried to persuade him to talk about himself, and was at last able to say tactfully that I understood he had no fiancée. He said that this was the case, and I said that no doubt one of his roving disposition was not naturally disposed to bind himself with home ties. He surprised me by saying that, on the contrary, he felt deeply the need for a home and a loved one. He reminded me that every bird has its nest and every expedition its base. He was in the unhappy position of being, as it were, an expedition without a base, a bird without a nest. During his wanderings he consoled his lonely heart with dreams of finding its desire. He liked to think that some day, over the brow of some distant hill, he would find his spiritual home; in a small but well-built cottage, with modern plumbing, he would find the soulmate who had waited faithfully for the lover she had dreamed of for so many lonely years. His wanderings, he said, were all *towards* somewhere; but where, he did not know; this was why he had sometimes been known to lose his way.

I said that I was touched by his confidence. I said I knew very well how he felt, having myself been a wanderer in my younger days. I asked Jungle whether he had never found a young lady to his taste. He said yes, he had found quite a number; in fact, he was always finding them. He said that, unfortunately, he lost them as quickly as he found them. He was in the habit of taking them on excursions on Saturday afternoons, and almost invariably mislaid them. He had lost three in succession on the South Downs. On the first occasion they had been overtaken by mist and Jungle had instructed his lady to remain where she was while he went for help. He took a northerly course until he reached a farm, then returned due south with a search party. The silly girl must have moved, for they were unable to find her. I asked him whether she had reached home safely. He said that he had not enquired; a girl who moved about in a mist against orders was hardly worth enquiring about. The next lady disappeared while Jungle was swinging his compass. The third became annoyed when Jungle inadvertently led her in a circle, and walked off. He had lost several in the Underground, two or three in Waterloo station, and any number in Hampton Court maze.

I made the friendly suggestion that next time, having found his lady, Jungle might keep hold of her and refrain from wandering. He said that he had often decided to do this, but it didn't seem to be in his nature. He was, he said, the victim of a Destiny. It was his Fate to go on finding his heart's desire and losing it, wandering about the face of the earth, forever homeless and lonely.

I said that this was the very stuff of Tragedy. It was so poetic that it must be true. I begged Jungle to think of himself as one chosen to fulfil a high and stern purpose; to put away weak desires and accept his Calling.

He thanked me and said that he would try to do as I suggested. He said that his earthly consolation should be that, himself a wanderer, he might sometimes be granted the privilege of guiding others.

At this point Pong brought his midday meal, and Jungle departed hurriedly for Camp 1 with his porter.

Left alone, I tried to meditate upon the responsibilities of leadership, but so weakened were my powers of concentration that I could think of nothing but apricot jam. Camp 1 was out of radio range, but in the evening I had a conversation with Wish, who had established Camp 4 at 33,000 feet. This was indeed good news; it cheered me so much that I was able, with no effort at all, to think of plum jam and marmalade. I asked Wish whether he liked plum jam. I think he thought I was light-headed.

11

Higher Still

I was sufficiently rested next day to set out for Camp 4, which was visible just below the skyline, a single small black dot in a white wilderness. I was now on the face of the mountain itself and the ground was steeper than it had been on the ridge and swept by an icy wind.

I moved slowly. My knees trembled; my feet turned to ten past ten; I frequently fell on my face. This, added to the fact that I no longer felt a strong desire to look for warples, led me to suspect that I was weakening. I found that my thoughts would rise no higher than my stomach or the next step, whichever was the lower. I was losing control of my destiny and the expedition.

This would never do. When the leader gives up the team falls to pieces. Who knew what struggles were going on below me? Was I to be the one to fail the party?

No, I said; I would not fail. I said it was time I stopped feeling sorry for myself. I had been telling myself that I was miserable, and, being a naturally truthful person, I had believed myself. The remedy was plain: I must tell myself something cheerful.

I told myself that my knees were firm and my feet straight. I told myself that I was gaining strength with every step. I said that my stomach-ache was hardly worth thinking about. I said I was all eagerness to find warples.

I talked to myself all day. I think I was on the point of convincing myself when, sometime in the late afternoon, I fancied my eyes were getting weak and began to fear snow-blindness. I told myself that it was all imagination. I tried hard to convince myself of this, and it did at last seem that my eyes were improving. But when we reached Camp 4 I found that my goggles had frosted over.

I found Wish in residence. He gave me a long and interesting list of the scientific apparatus he had seen during the previous day's climb. He kept me quite busy writing it all down. I would reproduce the list here; but it is not likely to be of general interest, being very like a manufacturer's catalogue.

I told Wish that I intended to spend one day at Camp 4 to acclimatize, then push on as quickly as possible in order to make maximum height before my strength gave out. I said I hoped he would accompany me.

Wish said that that was exactly what he himself would have liked to do. Unfortunately, he had deteriorated during his stay at Camp 4 and must go down to recuperate. He added that this would probably enable him, from Camp 3, to relay messages between myself at Camp 4 and those lower down. It was, he said, essential to make contact with the others, and this was the only practicable way of doing it.

I hope that I am not being self-indulgent when I ascribe to the effects of altitude my temporary irritation with Wish's logical conclusions. I recognized the truth of what he said, but it seemed to me at the time that Truth and Wish had ganged up against me. This was ungracious of me, particularly in view of Wish's sympathy in a similar situation at Camp 3.

After a frugal supper of lentils and pemmican I found myself sufficiently restored to make inner amends to Wish. This put me in the mood for a good talk, and, Wish being a scientist and used to dealing directly with truth, I saw no harm in confessing outright my interest in the matrimonial state of the party and asking him if he himself had a fiancée. He replied that it was an interesting point. I said yes, it was, and then we fell silent. After a while I reminded him that he had not answered my question and said I hoped he had not taken offence at anything I might have said. He said no, on the contrary; he was touched by my interest. The fact was, it was not quite clear to him either. I said I would be very happy if he would confide in me. He then told me his story, but slowly and with difficulty. Poor fellow, his emotion was so strong that the words did not come easily.

He had, he said, always wanted a fiancée. Even as a child it had been his heart's desire. He always asked Father Christmas to send him one, and repeated disappointments had caused him to develop at an early age a sense of disillusion which many a mature man might have envied. When he discovered that Father Christmas did not in fact exist he decided in his small mind that he could no longer place any trust in his parents. From this it was but a short step to doubting everything that was told him. By his sixth birthday he was a complete sceptic.

He asked me if I could understand his feelings. I said yes; a sensitive and intelligent child might easily react in this way. I myself had long had doubts about the advisability of Father Christmas, and Wish's experience was of great interest to me. I begged him to continue.

At the age of seven he asked his father to tell him the facts of life, with particular reference to fiancées. But he found it quite impossible to believe what was told him; it seemed to him, he said, much more unlikely than Father Christmas. In great bewilderment he consulted some of his small friends who, equally puzzled, approached their own parents on the subject. The explanations they brought to him were so varied and contradictory that the poor child was confirmed in his opinion that the whole thing was just another fairy-tale. He became convinced that fiancées were no more real than Father Christmas.

The parents of his small friends had become alarmed by the sudden outbreak of interest in this delicate subject. Having discovered the author, they held a meeting and, after much careful thought, they clubbed together and bought the boy a catapult, hoping that it would take his mind away from other things.

Except for the additional expense of broken windows they were quite satisfied with the result. The boy's natural delight at owning a weapon of destruction drew his attention away from the subject of fiancées, thus relieving an inner tension which might well have resulted in a political career.

Some years later, during his student days, his interest in the subject was reawakened by a chance remark made by a servant girl. By consulting works of reference and talking to many authorities he acquired an exhaustive knowledge of current beliefs. But his scepticism was still more robust than his credulity. In spite of a strong and self-confessed desire to believe he found it impossible to do so. It seemed, he said, that he alone of the human race was able to see the uncomfortable truth, to stand outside the cosy glow of illusion. He began to believe that his mission in life was to disclose to mankind the light which had revealed itself to him alone. He spoke eloquently and often in discussion and debate and founded a group known as 'Whence?' whose motto was 'Whither?' He even wrote a monograph entitled *Fiancées: The Pathetic Myth* which was published by the Sensible Press at 3½d. and remaindered in ten editions.

He was sent down from university for steadfastly refusing to believe anything which was taught him. The Whencians

gave him a public send-off and proclaimed him the first
martyr of the new lack of faith. But having come down he
found, as many a young man had found before him, that the
world of men and affairs was a vastly different place from the
world of his imaginings. His first rude awakening occurred
one Saturday afternoon in the saloon bar of *The Psychic
Psquirrel*. Wish had been holding forth in his usual way and
had, he thought, expounded his Theory of Scepticism with
particular clarity and brilliance. When he had finished, an
elderly, rather disreputable-looking gentleman of the eccentric type spoke a few quiet sentences which quite removed
Wish's self-satisfaction. He said he would not deny that
Wish showed certain faint glimmerings of promise as a
sceptic. But he had far to go. He must learn the elementary
truth that the real sceptic is sceptical by character rather than
conviction; the intellectual drapery in which he clothes his
scepticism has as little importance as the demonstrations of
the believer – it is, indeed, more likely to veil than to reveal
the naked Truth. Moreover, knowing that his mind will
enable him to doubt everything, the sceptic scorns the cru-
dity of *stating* his disbelief; he merely *lives* it. But even this,
the gentleman said, was going too far. The true sceptic
would refuse even to believe in himself and his own scepticism. He would maintain an openness of mind indistinguishable from complete mindlessness and an openness of
character indistinguishable from utter lack of character. His
scepticism would find its ultimate expression in the accept-
ance of random prejudice as being as sound a basis for living
as the most carefully reasoned philosophy. This, he said, was
the ultimate faith, for it scorned intellectual pretext. He said
that the true sceptic was far stronger in faith than any
believer.

Wish left *The Psychic Psquirrel* a very confused man. He

spent a wretched night and awoke with a violent headache
and a strong prejudice against alcoholic refreshment in any
form and casual conversation with eccentric strangers.

This prejudice was the turning-point in his life. There was,
he said, no arguing about it; sense or nonsense, it was completely convincing to him. This was a revelation. He reasoned
that since he must live by prejudice he might as well choose
the most comfortable ones he could find. He started to look
around him, scrutinizing carefully every prejudice he came
across, no matter how worn or dilapidated it might appear.
He examined thousands: some soft and comfortable, some
sharp and excruciating; prejudices large, prejudices small;
prejudices personal, national, harmless, deadly, ancient, modern, scientific, superstitious, plebeian, aristocratic, practical,
useless, orthodox, heretical: prejudices galore and free for the
taking. He felt, he said, like an explorer who comes upon a
treasure-chest crammed with the richest and most beautiful
gems.

He picked here and there, deliberately, taking his time. He
chose a complete set of prejudices which would last him a
lifetime and fit him to deal with any situation. He chose his
career. He joined a political party.

The pride of his collection was his old heart's desire: the
craving for a fiancée. Prejudice had restored what reason had
banished. Happily, reverently, with a feeling of miracles
performed, he put it back in its old place.

It didn't fit.

He turned it this way and that. He examined it for wear.
He reasoned with himself and read long passages from text
books. He lied to himself. He took advice from anybody
who would tell him what he wanted to hear.

All in vain!

Wish said he wondered if I could appreciate his feelings.

He had, he said, convinced himself beyond all reasonable doubt that the popular view was the correct one. He could prove it to himself by every known intellectual test. Moreover, he *wanted* to believe it. In a sense, he *did* believe it; but not completely. There was always a reserve at the back of his mind, and as time went on this emerged as a conviction that the whole thing was a plot to deceive him: a vast plot which included the writers of books and Wish's own friends.

He asked me if I thought him over-fanciful. I said that, on the contrary, I found it extremely interesting, having myself had an experience very similar to his, though perhaps less intense. It happened while I was on my way to Scotland to join some friends for a climbing holiday. Halfway up the Great North Road – I was travelling by bicycle – I began to suspect that Scotland did not exist: that it had been invented just to make a fool of me. All the books I had read, all the stories about thrifty Scotsmen, Shakespeare's Macbeth, Rabbie Burns, songs about Loch Lomond and Bonnie Charlie: all these were part of the conspiracy. The northerners who pretended to come from Scotland were all in the plot; their accent had been invented for the purpose. I was almost convinced that at Berwick-on-Tweed I should be laughed at by thousands of practical jokers whose entire lives had been devoted to bringing about this one ridiculous event. I became so apprehensive that I was unable to continue my journey by cycle. I thought that if I went by train I should avoid exposure; for if Scotland really did not exist the Railway Company would certainly know about it and would not issue a ticket. But when I got to the booking office I realized that if this was the case I should look just as foolish trying to buy a ticket as if I tried to cycle to Scotland – with no possible chance of pretending that I had really no intention of going further than the border. I realized too that if there actually was a conspiracy the Railway Company would be in it and would have false tickets ready at every booking office in case I came along. But it was too late to turn back. I bought a ticket to Berwick, and was almost sure that the clerk looked disappointed. Once on the train I made discreet enquiries of officials and my fellow travellers, besides examining labels in the luggage van, and decided that if it was all part of the conspiracy it was a remarkably thorough business. I decided that Scotland was a calculated risk worth taking. At Berwick I left the train and cycled over the border.

Wish said that this was exactly the sort of thing he had experienced in regard to fiancées. Unfortunately, he had been able to find no easy solution such as mine. Shortly after the encounter at *The Psychic Psquirrel* he met a young person who, he said, was exactly the kind of person he would have wished to have as a fiancée if he could have persuaded himself to believe in them. So strong were his feelings that he decided to risk exposure by asking her to be his. To his great delight she promised to do so.

This occurred just before we left England. For a few days Wish was the happiest mountaineer alive. His dearest childhood dream was realized. He was almost ready to believe in Father Christmas.

Then came Doubt. *Was* it true? *Could* it be true? Was his fiancée, perhaps, in the conspiracy? Would he, on our return home, be exposed to a nation's ridicule?

Since then he had been torn between Love and Fear, and had not known a moment's peace. Nobody, he said, could possibly imagine the torments he had borne.

He groaned in a most distressing way. Poor fellow! I tried to reassure him that his fears were all fancies; but what could I do against the scepticism of a lifetime? I told him I would not be happy until I had put his mind at ease. I begged him to let me share his thoughts and help him in his struggle. He was pathetically grateful, but would not hear of it. I had, he said, enough responsibility already. He must bear his burden as best he could and face the issue manfully on his return to England. He thanked me for listening to him, but said that it would make it easier for him if we did not refer to the matter again. I promised, but with a lump in my throat, and vowed to myself that I would think less about my own troubles in future.

12

Not High Enough

Next morning saw the departure of Wish for Camp 3.
After he had left I lay in my sleeping-bag thinking over
his unhappy story. How strange, I thought, that all my companions – with the possible exception of Shute, with whom I
had not yet had the opportunity to talk – had had such unexpected and melancholy experiences. How little one suspected of the secrets locked in the human breast! How seldom
did one guess that the cheerful smile hid a breaking heart!
This, I resolved, should be a lesson I would not forget: that
we are all team-mates in suffering. I resolved that never again
would I judge a person by his exterior, no matter how impenetrable or forbidding it might appear.

At that moment Pong entered with my breakfast. When I
looked at his impenetrable exterior I realized that he, too,
was just a human being, after all. Who knew what agony
and desolation lay behind his flat and forbidding exterior?
While suffering breakfast I thought about this. Had we, perhaps, been unkind to Pong? Poor fellow, he was the outcast
of the expedition. Nobody seemed to like him. Was he, perhaps, intolerably lonely? Was he aching for a kind word or
a smile?

It was almost too sad to think about. I put my breakfast
aside and went to Pong's tent. I found him filing a fork into
a bowl. He took no notice of me. After a while he laid down
the fork and began to grate a piece of rock. I thought I had
better let him get used to my presence before trying to com-

municate with him; so I sat down and watched him. After chopping up a portion of climbing rope and mincing an old sock he threw everything into a pan of pemmican stew and stirred for five minutes, adding sand and paraffin to taste. Finally, he strained it, spread some of it on a slice of leather, and took a hearty bite.

This, I thought, was my opportunity. Drawing his attention by a cough, I pointed to the leather and to my mouth.

At first he did not seem to grasp my meaning. I repeated the gesture, then made motions of mastication, smiled, and rubbed my stomach. His hand came slowly forward, as though he was still not sure what I wanted. I took the leather from him, bit off a small piece and returned it to him.

We chewed in silence. I let the situation consolidate itself for a few minutes, then I coughed again. To my great delight Pong coughed too! I turned one of his pans upside down and, with the point of a fork, drew on the dirty bottom a rough picture of a Yogistani fiancée. I pointed to Pong and to the drawing, and raised my eyebrows.

He didn't seem to understand. I kept on raising my eyebrows, and suddenly he started doing the same. He put his face quite close to mine and raised his eyebrows in time with my own.

I held my ground, and we went on like this for some time. I did not like to stop, fearing to hurt his feelings.

Then something strange happened to his face: something quite indescribable, like nothing I had ever seen before or imagined possible. I stared, fascinated. What could it be?

Then I knew. It was a smile!

I admit freely that I was touched. That Pong's forbidding exterior should break into a smile seemed almost like a miracle. What undreamed-of emotions could be the cause of it? With great eagerness I set about finding out.

I will not weary the reader with an account of the steps by which Pong and I developed our sign-language and came at last to understand each other. Such a thing might well seem impossible; but, as I have often had occasion to remark: good will is the best interpreter.

I told him about my family and described my home. I spoke warmly of our English cooking methods, and gave him one or two recipes. In return he showed me how to fry rubber, and told me that he was a graduate of the University of Yogistan, where he had taken a third degree in cookery. At last, after some hours of persistence – for he had a tendency to chatter about trifles – I got him to tell me about his fiancée.

He had never wanted a fiancée. He had, he said, the artistic temperament, which he held to be incompatible with the sentiments and behaviour proper to one betrothed. He wished me to understand that he had nothing against the opposite sex – quite the contrary – but his artistic soul re-belled against the regimentation necessary to official engage-ment. Unfortunately, it is the Yogistani custom for children to be betrothed at an early age by parental arrangement. Thus, Pong was firmly engaged long before his artistic tem-perament showed itself, and when it finally did it found itself immediately at loggerheads with society, with his fam-ily and with his fiancée. Pong had always had a horror of loggerheads; his sensitive soul was intimately tuned to the most subtle nuances of social intercourse. Finding himself now at what appeared to be permanent and irreconcilable loggerheads with his fellow-creatures, in general and in the nearest particular, he underwent a spiritual crisis. As he saw it, he must choose once and for all between his art and his heart; he could be either an artist or a lover, but not both. The conflict was terrible. Pong told me that nobody could possibly have the slightest idea of what he went through. He had, until that time, been willing to accept his fiancée, and genuinely fond of his family and friends. Now, his deepest and most imperative urge was to abandon them all to follow the lonely path of his calling.

For months he lived in an agony of indecision. It seemed that his soul was being torn in two. Then one day something occurred which forced him to a decision. He was spending Saturday afternoon, as usual, at the home of his fiancée, who on these occasions was in the habit of preparing some special delicacy for her beloved. He sat down to table, grasped his chopsticks firmly in his right hand, placed his left hand on his hip, and assumed an expression of pleasant anticipation. The lady walked in proudly and placed a dish before him.

The next moment, Pong uttered a cry of horror and flung the bowl from him. The poor lady laid a hand on his arm, but he brushed her aside and rushed from the house.

All day and all night he paced the mountainside. In the morning he came down a changed – and a dedicated – man. From that morning he had devoted himself to his art. His fiancée, his family, his friends forsook him; he was un-compromising, and no one loved him sufficiently to under-stand and to accept second place in his affections. He became an outcast; not willingly or wilfully, for he was a sociable soul, but because the artist must tread his own unfrequented heights.

And as his skill increased and his insight sharpened, his desire for companionship increased also, until it was well-nigh intolerable. Yet the very strength of his longing was an added barrier between himself and his fellows; on the few occasions when he had revealed it the would-be friend had been appalled by its intensity. He became lonelier than ever.

At last he gave up the effort to reach his fellow-men. He retired completely into his inner world and poured all the vigour of his affections into his art. After taking his degree he made his own experiments and founded a new school of cookery which was acclaimed by the radical element throughout the country as the embodiment of the spirit of the age. He became universally respected and honoured, but never loved.

And now, he said, his life's work was done. He would never climb higher than he had already climbed. The rest would be mere repetition. Younger men must stand on his shoulders. For him, there remained gratitude to life for making use of him, the determination to grow old gracefully, and, deep and inextinguishable as ever, the human hope that he might yet find the affection of an equal.

*

That, if I understood him correctly, was Pong's story. For some minutes after he finished there was stillness in the little tent. Neither of us spoke a gesture. Then, with the sigh of one who returns to earth after an excursion into dreams, Pong drew out his pouch and offered me a pipeful of *stunk*. Too full for signs, I whispered a heartfelt: 'No thank you, old chap,' and hurried from the tent.

Back in my own tent I spat out the leather and got into my sleeping-bag. I lay a long time thinking about Pong's strange story and trying to imagine what the sign-language for 'maestro' might be. The expedition seemed very far away and everything connected with it strangely unreal. But at last I roused myself to a sense of my responsibilities. Where were the others? What should my own movements be?

A sharp twinge about the middle provided part of the answer. It was no use trying to pretend that I had no stomach-ache. A friendly Pong was not likely to be any more acceptable as a cook than he had been before. My dyspepsia tablets had run out. Unless help reached me soon I was lost.

I seized the walkie-talkie and buzzed. To my delight I made contact with Wish, who was at Camp 3. He had already been speaking to Constant and Shute, who had advanced to Camp 2. Burley and Jungle were still at Camp 1.

This was excellent news. The whole party could at last be united by radio. We soon discovered that I was out of range of Camp 2; I could speak to them only via Wish. Wish, likewise, could not reach Camp 1; his conversation with them must be relayed via Camp 2. I asked Wish to arrange for Constant to stand by at Camp 2 and Burley at Camp 1. While he was doing so I tried to make plans for the assault on the summit, still 7,000 feet above me. But the only plans I was able to make were connected with my stomach. I decided that dyspepsia tablets must be sent up at once, by porter, from the medical store at Camp 1.

When Wish called me again his voice was very faint, and I raised my own voice, asking him to speak up. Instead of doing so he became even fainter. I learnt afterwards that I was speaking too loudly and he, as one does in such cases, dropped his own voice instinctively. He was now almost inaudible to me, and I shouted as loudly as I could, which quite saturated his receiver and nearly deafened him. Neither of us could understand a word the other was saying. We might have given it up in despair had I not, while pausing to recover my breath, overheard Wish telling Constant that I was shouting his head off. This put me right, and soon Wish was able to tell me that they were all standing by.

But just as I was about to speak the radio began to crackle. From that moment we had the greatest difficulty in making ourselves understood. To make matters worse we forgot, in our enthusiasm, Jungle's careful training, and spoke as in ordinary conversation. The result was as follows:

MYSELF to Wish: Tell Burley to send six packets of number eights to Camp 4.

WISH to Constant: Tell Burley to send six packets of Weights to Camp 4.

MYSELF (who had overheard this): Not dates; *eights*.

WISH: I didn't say plates.

MYSELF: I didn't say you did.

CONSTANT to Wish: What do you mean, you didn't say crates? I know you didn't; you said packets.

WISH: No! No! I was talking to Binder. He says *not* dates. Or was it plates? Anyway, he doesn't want them.

MYSELF: But I *do* want them.

WISH to Constant: He says he does want them, after all.

CONSTANT: Wants what?

WISH: Why . . . er . . . just a minute! Binder: was it dates or plates?

MYSELF: Oh dear!

WISH to Constant: He says he wants some cold beer.

CONSTANT: Well, he knows we haven't got any. Is he light-headed, do you think?

MYSELF: *Not* beer! *Not* beer!

WISH to Constant: I think he must be. He says he wants some hot beer now.

CONSTANT: This is serious. He must be delirious. Ask him if he knows Burley.

WISH: Binder, Applecart wants to know if you rose early.

CONSTANT: Not Curly, you fool! *Burley*.

WISH: I didn't say Shirley.

MYSELF to Wish: I know you didn't.

CONSTANT to Wish: I didn't say you did.

WISH: WILL EVERYBODY PLEASE KEEP
   QUIET WHILE I GO GENTLY MAD.
BURLEY to Constant: What's going on, Applecart? Why
   are you talking nonsense?
CONSTANT: There's no wonder. Binder and Fiddler have
   gone off their heads.
BURLEY: Lost their beds?
CONSTANT: NO!
WISH to Constant: What on earth are you raving about?
   Can't you keep quiet while I try to think?
CONSTANT to Wish: If you want to think, turn off your
   ruddy receiver.
BURLEY to Constant: Who on earth wants to think? What
   are you talking about?
MYSELF to Wish: I didn't say anything. Are you sure you
   feel all right?
WISH: I FEEL AWFUL.

This was bad enough. But so far we had managed to syn-
chronize our switching so that when A was speaking B was
listening, and vice versa. Now we fell out of step. A and B
would both be speaking and neither listening. Quite probably we were all speaking together at some time or other
with nobody listening at all. For a long time it was chaos. I
am sure that before very long we should have driven each
other really mad, or at least that our faith in the rationality of
human behaviour and man's control of his own destiny
would have been seriously damaged. But we were spared
this. Into our bedlam broke a voice: a lovely, controlled,
pedantic, competent voice:

   'Wanderer to Applecart. Wanderer to Applecart. Are you
receiving me? Over.... Wanderer to Applecart. Wanderer
to Applecart. Are you receiving me? Over....'

Constant says that it came to him like the voice of a
Superior Being. Through the crackling and distortion the
familiar phrases rang clear and unmistakable. The monotonous chant which had seemed so strange when we re-
hearsed at Base Camp pushed like a bulldozer through the
disturbance; the ear, not having to chase up and down, was
able to ignore the interference. And the message left him in
no doubt as to who was speaking to whom.

Constant took up the ritual joyfully:

'Applecart to Wanderer. Applecart to Wanderer. Receiving you loud and clear....'

Wish, hearing him, put me right too, and our planning
was soon proceeding smoothly. Burley promised to send off
the number eights first thing in the morning. He and Jungle
were uncertain as to their state of fitness and would remain
at Camp 1 a little longer. Constant and Shute would stay at
Camp 2 to rest after their climb. Wish would stay at Camp
3. This arrangement would keep open the radio contact. I
decided that since the stomach tablets could not reach me before evening next day I might as well do a day's work while
I was still strong enough to climb. I would go as high as I
could, dump the equipment for Camp 5, and return to
Camp 4.

*

I spent a restless night and rose unrested. Pong, when he
brought my breakfast, was as inscrutable as ever, except that
he allowed a powerful belch to escape him – a thing which
had never occurred before. I wondered whether he had begun to take advantage of my sympathy; but rebuked myself
immediately for the uncharitable thought.

When I summoned So Lo he, too, belched at me. This, if
not a conspiracy, was a remarkable coincidence. I decided to
keep my ears open in future. It is not pleasant to suspect that

one has been taken advantage of. Apart from one's desire not to be thought a fool, or to think oneself one, one never knows whether to despise the other person for having taken mean advantage, or oneself for suspecting him without justification. It was with mixed feelings that I began the day's climb.

It was not long before my feelings were a good deal more mixed. I let So Lo take the lead as usual – it would, in fact, have been difficult to prevent him – and fell victim immediately to Binder's Butter Beans, which had attached themselves to the tune of 'Let us with a Gladsome Mind' and were ten times as persistent as before. Besides fighting the Beans, I was trying to plan for the future. I was also trying to keep an eye open for warples and hallucinations and an ear for belches.

I was experiencing new and startling pains about the waistline, and the labour of climbing and breathing was getting more difficult. My mind began to wander. It seemed at one time that my companions had brought their fiancées and families with them; somewhere below me was a struggling crowd of people: Prone with his nasty wife and awful children, Burley and his unfortunate fiancée, Constant and Travers – singing sea-chanties – Jungle and his host of lost loves, and poor Wish with the fiancée he could not quite believe in. They were all my dear friends – even Prone's family – and I told myself I must make an effort for their sake. 'Come on, Binder!' I said to myself. But it was more easily said than done. It was no use trying to convince myself that I had no stomach-ache. My character was, I realized, already weakened by the lies I had told myself during the last climb. To deceive oneself was folly and cowardice. I must face up to the truth and accept it gladly. To accept truth was to accept life, and life itself would reward me.

So I started on my stomach-ache and tried to be happy

about it. Let my pain, I said, be my offering to life and to friendship. I would bear it happily for Pong's sake.

That sounded very nice, but it wouldn't work if I suspected Pong of taking advantage. For the sake of the expedition I must believe in Pong. After all, I told myself, Yogistani is spoken from the stomach; those belches might well be Yogistani for 'good-morning'.

So I put away my suspicions and tried to gather Pong and the others, and my stomach-ache, and all the rest of my troubles, into a single ecstasy. 'I will live!' I cried, and fell flat on my face.

I picked myself up and added a painful nose to my ecstasy. Aching with joy I forced myself on and up. And step by step the going became easier. I was thrilled to find myself climbing as I had not climbed for days. Had I found the secret of life and energy? The slope seemed barely perceptible; it was almost as though we were walking on level ground.

I raised my head and looked around me. We *were* on level ground!

I walked on a few steps and bumped into So Lo, who had stopped. I stood still, regaining my breath, then looked ahead, wondering what obstacles might be waiting for us.

To my utter astonishment, there were no obstacles.

We were on the summit!

For the second time on the expedition I doubted my own sanity. Rum Doodle was 40,000½ feet high. Unless either my barometer or myself was mad, we were at 35,000. What could have happened?

Then I saw. Over to the east a magnificent mountain stood against the sky, its glittering summit 5,000 feet above me.

We had climbed the wrong mountain.

13

It Goes !

Very small and lonely I felt as I shivered in the biting wind on the summit of North Doodle. The majestic summit of Rum Doodle towered above me, scarcely more than a mile distant; but between us the Conundra gorge plunged to awful and unseen depths.

My thoughts went back to that evening, which seemed an eternity ago, when we had stood on the summit of the Rankling La, our hearts beating with hope, eager to challenge the mountain. All the effort, the suffering, the planning, had been in vain. The confidence of those who had chosen us was betrayed. We were failures and frauds; the world would laugh at us, and rightly.

I thought of my comrades below, struggling against bodily weakness, building up their strength for the work which they imagined lay ahead, forcing their way up the mountain slowly but valiantly, and all to no purpose. It seemed infinitely pathetic. A lump rose in my throat and I fought back unmanly tears.

I looked up at the summit of Rum Doodle, so serene in its inviolate purity, and I had the fancy that the goddess of the mountain was looking down with scorn upon the puny creatures who had set sacrilegious feet upon her slopes, daring them to do their utmost, daring the whole world. She it was who had led us astray, and would lead astray or destroy all who set foot on her.

Would the mountain ever be climbed, I wondered.

And as I looked I had the answer.

On the broad slopes of the summit a small black speck had appeared. As I watched, it moved slowly upwards. Behind it came another speck. Then another.

Men!

Who could it be, upon our mountain? I felt a surge of indignation. Who had dared to come to the mountain in secret, to beat us to the summit and make fools of us? Who?

The three specks moved upwards. Behind them appeared other specks, in ones and twos and larger groups. There were ten of them, twenty, dozens, scores; the virgin whiteness of the summit snow was dotted with them. They swarmed all over it, like slow-moving ants.

The porters! It could be no one else. Ninety-two had been left at Base Camp. They must all, or nearly all, have climbed the mountain.

But why? Why?

And where was Prone? Was he with them, or had he been abandoned? Had he led them himself?

I seized my radio. The distance was beyond normal range, but contact might be possible in this clear air. I buzzed and called:

'Binder to Ailing. Binder to Ailing. Are you receiving me? Over.'

No reply. I tried again, and went on trying. I became frantic.

So Lo and Pong were seated placidly on their loads, smoking *stunk* and watching their friends on Rum Doodle with no sign of interest. It seemed to be all in a day's work to them. The specks on the summit were working in groups. Tents were being erected. They were evidently going to camp on the mountain top!

I went on calling.

At last, to my great relief, there came a faint voice:

'Ailing to Binder. Ailing to Binder. Receiving you strength 2. Are you receiving me? Over.'

And he told me his incredible story. On the day Constant and I left Advanced Base for the last time the porters had started to pack up all the equipment which we had left at Base Camp. When everything else was ready they pulled his tent down too and indicated by signs that he was to get out of his sleeping-bag. Assuming that they were carrying out Constant's orders to move the camp to a safer site, he did as requested, and they moved off in good order, Prone, who was suffering from suspected catalepsy, being carried by a porter on top of his load.

To his surprise, instead of making for the chosen site they marched straight to the North Wall and began to climb it. He shouted and wriggled, but the porter who was carrying him took not the slightest notice. He kicked and bellowed, and banged the fellow on the head with his fist. The man bore it for a while, then threw Prone off and went on alone. Greatly alarmed, Prone staggered after him, calling on him to stop. The porter halted, waited for Prone to come up, flung him over his shoulder and went on again. Prone, quite demoralized, made himself as comfortable as he could and fell asleep.

He awoke to find himself being carried into his tent. From a brief glimpse which he caught of the surroundings he guessed that they were encamped on the South Col. He was given food and his personal equipment was brought to him. After treating himself for Bavarian measles he turned in for the night.

Next morning they struck camp and Prone with it. Taking no notice whatsoever of his expostulations, the same porter threw him on top of his load, and off they went again.

And they kept hard at it, day after day, until they reached the summit. Prone said that he had never been so miserable in his life. The things he had endured, he said, would make a strong colonial turn pale by the mere telling. Rum Doodle was a far stiffer mountain than he had ever, in his most pessimistic moments, dreamed. He was carried all the way by the same porter, whose name was Un Sung.

I sympathized with him, and gave him my news. We then considered what was to be done. Obviously, Prone and the Base Camp must be got down the mountain. But how? At my suggestion Prone tried, by signs, to persuade his gang to go downhill, but they took no notice of him. They had by now finished pitching the tents. Those not engaged in preparing food were sitting inside smoking and apparently quite contented with their unusual situation. Prone said it was hopeless.

I said I could not imagine how the thing had happened. Prone said that he, on the other hand, knew exactly. The Yogistani word for mountain base was evidently the same as the word for summit, except for a grunt, gurgle or other internal convulsion which Constant had got wrong. In his opinion the porters would stay where they were until told by Constant to come down, or until supplies gave out. He expected to be dead long before either of these happened.

I begged him to bear up, for all our sakes. I told him that his sufferings had not been for nothing. Had we not, after all, reached the summit of Rum Doodle? We had, in fact, accomplished far more than we had set out to do, having climbed both Rum and North Doodle.

Prone said that, in years to come, if ever he sat again in comfort before a blazing fire, this fact might be of some small satisfaction to him. At present it was a raindrop in his ocean of misery. He begged me to get him off the mountain.

To comfort the poor fellow I promised that this would be done at once; though how, I had not the faintest idea. We said good-bye, and I started downhill with my small party.

*

At Camp 4 I found my precious packets of stomach tablets. I called up Wish and told him the news. I said I would go down to Camp 2 next day and Camp 1 the day after. I took a frugal supper and turned in early. So Lo and Pong both came and belched at me, and I hoped they were only saying 'good-night'.

It was a pair of belches which woke me next morning. I looked at them both suspiciously, but Pong had brought a piece of leather for me to eat with my lentils and pemmican. I took this to be a friendly gesture and was ashamed of my suspicions.

I can remember little of the next two days except my continual struggle with Binder's Butter Beans. At 27,000 feet I called up the others and asked them to direct me to Camp 1. They were very helpful, but their detailed instructions did nothing but lead me in a circle. But it was good to hear Burley's voice again. In the background, as he spoke, I could hear the sound of singing, and now and then someone would break into our conversation with a friendly enquiry, such as: 'How's old Binder today?' or 'Binder, old boy, did I ever tell you the story of the Young Lady from Kettering?' and so on. Burley himself offered to sing for me. It was very kind of them, and after my lonely journey I was touched; but it was no help to me in my search for Camp 1.

At last I gave it up. I said I would go down to Advanced Base, and asked them to follow next day. Burley consulted the others and I heard Shute say: 'We might as well; there's none left, anyway,' – meaning cinematograph film, I suppose.

I have since discussed with Totter the mystery of Camp 1. Why was I never able to find it, in spite of repeated instructions? Why had Constant been able to find it easily when he went down from Camp 2? And why did the others, notably Burley, who never went higher, find it so difficult to leave the camp? Was it a local climatic effect similar to the enervating air one often finds on a glacier? We never found a satisfactory explanation. To this day the mystery of Camp 1 remains unsolved.

So down I went to Advanced Base, and one day later we were all together for the first time for nearly a fortnight.

The question was: what was to be done about Prone? Jungle's telescope revealed that Base Camp was still pitched on the summit. A dark cloud which hung over it was doubtless the smoke from ninety-two pipes of *stunk*. Did they intend to stay there, as Prone feared, until ordered down or food ran out? Constant consulted the porters, who assured him that this was undoubtedly the case. Orders, they said, were orders; and these particular orders had been to take Base Camp to the summit and wait there for the rest of the expedition.

Clearly, someone would have to be sent after them. But who? Since none of the Europeans was fit to try we must send porters. Constant asked for volunteers, with disappointing results. He picked out two of them and ordered them up. After a haggle about overtime rates they packed their loads and set off at once without a sign of enthusiasm or reluctance. It was all in a day's work to them.

The South Col was no place for a group of tired mountaineers. Next day we descended to the glacier and set up our camp at the foot of the North Wall.

We waited.

14

Return of the Summit Party

We rested first, having our sleep out. Then, with returning energy, we became active again, each in his own way. Wish collated his many readings and announced with pride that they were proving of the greatest importance. Jungle was profitably employed in surveying the area. Unfortunately, he lost himself every day and had to be rescued at great inconvenience to the rest of us. This became so irksome that we appointed a porter to be his guardian, giving him strict instructions to bring Jungle back to camp at dusk. One evening they had not returned by nightfall and Shute sent up a number of flares – brought for photographic purposes – to guide them. One of the flares fell on Wish's tent and burned it to the ground, together with his records. Wish was distracted. All his work had gone up in flames. Having boiled all the mercury out of his thermometers he could take no more readings, and the remainder of his equipment was on the summit of Rum Doodle. He had been unable to find any living creature on the mountain; this line of research also had come to nothing. There was only one hope of justifying his presence: he must concentrate all his energies on the search for warples. Since Shute had no work of his own – all his film being spoiled and his lenses cracked – Wish conscripted him for the search. Burley was also enlisted. He was now fully acclimatized and as fit and active as a schoolboy, and fairly wore out both Wish and Shute on the daily warple-hunt.

Constant, insatiable as ever in his desire to improve his knowledge of the language, spent much time with the porters. At other times he was to be found wandering about the glacier practising grunts, gurgles and the other phenomena which are the backbone of spoken Yogistani. It was the general opinion, he said, that Yogistani was unpronounceable to the Western stomach, and it was his great ambition to prove that this was a fallacy. He was, he told me, within hearing of success. He had developed unmistakable symptoms of the permanent gastritis which is hypodermic amongst the Yogistani due to their speaking from the stomach. Burley was unkind enough to suggest that if Constant had developed his stomach-ache at the right time Prone would not now be marooned on the summit of Rum Doodle. I reminded him that but for this accident we would have failed in our purpose, and I congratulated Constant on his gastritis. It was, by the way, interesting to notice that as this complaint increased in severity Constant became more and more immune to the effects of Pong's cooking, and began even to enjoy it. He put forward the theory that the Yogistani method of cooking provides a counter-irritant to the indigenous indigestion pains. However that might be, it seemed to work in his case. It was unfortunate that on returning to civilization he found himself quite unable to stomach Western cooking. For weeks he lived on a starvation diet while he experimented with every conceivable mixture of ill-assorted foodstuffs and every possible method of rendering them indigestible. Finally, when on the verge of committing suicide by eating pre-digested invalid food, he conceived the happy idea of employing a Yogistani cook. He at once sent off cables in all directions, one of which, by great good fortune, reached Pong. Owing to the difficulty of transmitting grunts, gurgles and so on by cable, as well as to objections by Pong's trade union, the negotiations were prolonged, and Constant nearly succumbed to indigestion complicated by excitement. But matters were arranged at last. Pong is now installed in Constant's Hampstead flat. Almost any time of day they may be found grunting and gurgling together in the kitchen as they gloat over some malevolent mess which is burning on the bottom of a disgusting saucepan, or huddled in ecstasy over bowls of the same atrocity. When I last saw him Constant was smoking a pipe of *stunk* which, he found, served the same purpose of counter-irritant as Pong's cooking.

But I anticipate. During this anxious time at Base Camp, when the fate of poor Prone was as yet unknown to us, I was once more heartened and inspired by the devoted way in which my companions went about their tasks, allowing no personal grief to interfere with duty. I forced myself to take my part in all activities, social and otherwise, and found that in helping to lighten the burden of others I had also eased my own.

I had for some time been eager to learn something about Shute's fiancée; but now that opportunity presented itself I was at a loss how to broach the subject, not knowing what tender susceptibilities might be involved. One afternoon I was sitting alone in the mess tent, composing a letter of condolence for Prone's father, when Shute strolled in. He was, he said, at a loose end. Did I mind if he showed me some snaps? I said I should be delighted. He produced several photographs of a nice-looking young lady whom he said was his fiancée. They were to be married soon after his return. I congratulated him and wished him every happiness. He thanked me. I said that his fiancée looked a very nice young lady. He said she was the nicest and dearest person in the world. He told me quite a lot about her and it all sounded very happy and very normal. He asked me if he was boring me. I said no, but was there not some drawback to his happiness? He said no, why should there be? I said it often happened; perhaps he had had unhappy experiences before meeting this fiancée. He said no; they had been childhood sweethearts; there had never been anyone else; why did I ask? I said that somehow I had expected something different. He looked at me rather suspiciously, I thought, and said he was sorry to disappoint me. I at once assured him that he had mistaken my meaning and asked him to tell me more, which he did, and more than satisfied my curiosity. His fiancée was evidently as normal and contented a person as he was himself; I could see that they would have a very happy life together. I asked him what they did on Saturday afternoons. He told me that they visited his fiancée's elderly aunt, who was bed-ridden.

I noticed that the daily belch with which Pong and So Lo greeted me on the mountain had spread to the other porters. I asked Constant if he knew what it meant. He said that since Yogistani was spoken from the stomach the belch – the stomach's sign of ultimate contentment – was used as an expression of respect; it indicated the great pleasure which the belcher found at being in the illustrious presence of the belchee.

This pleased me greatly, not only because I appreciated the honour, but because it confirmed my faith in Pong and in human nature. I wished that time and my duties would allow me to make friends with each of the porters. What a wealth of affection must, I thought, be hidden by their unresponsive manner. I spent much time with Pong, who told me many interesting things about his life. Poor fellow, he seemed to have developed a great affection for me. He told Constant that I was the only person who had ever been kind to him without expecting something in return. This touched me deeply. He also developed the habit of bringing me little offerings of food at all hours of the day. This touched me deeply too.

*

After some days of careful thought I sent off the following despatch: 'Expedition more than successful, having climbed both Doodles. All in good health and spirits. The spirit of the team is excellent and the porters are beyond praise.'

I inadvertently signed this message 'Binder' instead of with my proper name. This caused some perplexity at home, and the despatch was at first considered to be a hoax. Then the rumour went round that we had been forestalled on the mountain by an unknown party under the leadership of one, Binder. Enquiries were made in mountaineering circles, but no clue could be found. The affair caused considerable excitement, the national press making the most of it, and was not cleared up until our arrival at Chaikhosi, where we were inundated with telegrams from all parts of the world and had to employ three secretaries to deal with them. One of the secretaries turned out to be a practical joker named Pluke, who made the most of an unparalleled opportunity and had the world's press at its wits end by issuing foolish and contradictory statements. We had to employ six extra secretaries to clear up the confusion he caused.

But again I anticipate. As the days passed and no sign was seen of Prone I became more and more worried. Heaven alone knew what torments the poor fellow was enduring – if, indeed, he was still alive. At last I could stand it no longer. I called the others to the mess tent and said that something must be done. Someone must go up the mountain. The question was: who? All looked at each other, but no one spoke.

This made me feel very humble. 'My dear chaps,' I said, 'I know you all want to go; but someone must stay behind. I feel it my responsibility. I hope you won't consider it selfish if I go.'

There was silence. Then Burley looked at me keenly and said, in his deep voice: 'By heavens, Binder, I believe you would!'

I looked at him in surprise. He seemed, for some reason, to be overcome by emotion.

'If you go,' he said at last, 'I go!'

At that moment the tent door was flung open, and in walked Prone.

*

A new Prone.

An erect Prone.

A thin but healthy-looking Prone.

A Prone with a broad smile and a swagger.

Prone, the hero of Rum Doodle; the man who had been higher than anyone else; for, as Wish pointed out, Prone stood head and shoulders higher than any of the porters.

What a reunion that was! What laughter! What back-slapping! What wrestling and practical jokes!

When we were all exhausted Prone said: 'As medical officer to this expedition I prescribe champagne. Where's the medical equipment?'

At this a silence fell upon us. The others looked sheepish and nudged each other to speak. At last, Burley said:

'The fact is, old boy, there *is* no champagne.'

'No champagne!' Prone was horrified.

'No. You see, we ... er ... didn't bring it back from Camp 1.'

But nothing could dampen our spirits that day. In the absence of a more stimulating beverage cocoa was made. We were soon laughing again, telling and retelling our adventures. Everybody wanted to talk, none to listen.

'Do you remember,' said Shute, smiling, 'how Binder got stuck to the glacier by his tears?'

'And had Pong all to himself for a week,' said Wish, chuckling.

'And couldn't find Camp 1,' laughed Jungle.

'And had to have number eights sent up,' added Constant, holding his sides.

We all roared.

All of a sudden, Burley jumped up.

'Stop it!' he cried.

He banged on the table.

The laughter stopped at once. The mood changed instantaneously. We waited in tense silence for Burley to speak. Wish giggled nervously, then coughed and turned red.

Burley was frowning. His fist thumped the table. He seemed to be struggling with words.

'There's something that needs saying,' he said at last. Then he fell silent again, and again we waited.

'A lot of things,' he continued, 'have happened on this expedition – and before it started – which seemed very appropriate at the time.'

He stopped again. He was evidently choosing his words carefully. He banged on the table. 'I wish now they had never happened.'

What on earth, I wondered, was the dear fellow talking about?

'I myself,' he was saying, 'have been as guilty as anyone else – probably more so.'

I noticed that the others were exchanging glances and looking sheepish again. What *was* it all about?

'Just now,' Burley went on, 'old Binder here was about to

go to Prone's rescue. Let's not forget that. Let's not forget also that Binder had already done ten times as much work as the rest of us put together and carried the whole responsibility for the climb. He had already been to 35,000 feet while we were wallowing at Camp 1. Yet *he* was the chap who was going to climb Rum Doodle to bring Prone back.'

This was embarrassing. We had all done our best. I had perhaps been more fortunate than the others; but the luck might easily have been different. I tried to interrupt Burley, but he put his hand on my shoulder.

'No,' he said. 'Let me finish.'

He looked at the others, each in turn.

'I will now, gentlemen,' he said, 'propose the health of our leader: the most conscientious, the most modest, the most unselfish man I have ever climbed with.

'And,' he added, 'he has more guts than any of us.'

And those absurd fellows drank my health in cocoa.

The next moment they were all trying to shake my hand at the same time, while Prone was patting my back and saying: 'Well done, little man!'

It was quite ridiculous. To this day I am not sure whether it was another of Burley's feeble jokes.

15

Farewell to Rum Doodle

Next day we checked our stores and found that the porters had eaten nearly all the food, leaving only a few bags of butter beans. This was serious. We could not feed the porters another day; they must be dismissed at once. We decided to retain one porter only to carry our food for the return journey. We must abandon all our equipment, keeping only the most necessary personal effects, such as alarm clocks and hot-water bottles.

Constant addressed the porters and, after much excitement, told us that they understood the position. They insisted, however, on being paid up to the probable date of our arrival at Chaikhosi, Since to argue with them would mean feeding them for several days there seemed nothing else to do. We paid them and told them to be off. But instead of going they all came and stood in front of my tent, where I was cutting my toe nails. When I went out to see what they wanted, Bing came forward and stood in front of me. He looked me straight in the eye and uttered a powerful belch. Then he walked away. Bung followed him, then Bo, then So Lo and Lo Too; then all of them. One by one they came and belched at me. The glacier echoed with belches – from the deep bass rumble of Bing to the treble peeps of the boys. Burley said it reminded him of Aldershot. One little fellow seemed to be stomach-tied. He stood in front of me shyly, unable to produce a sound. Then he made a kind of cough and ran off amidst laughter.

Last of all came Pong. Poor fellow, the tears were stream-
ing down his face. His magnificent belch brought a murmur
of approval and admiration from all present. We embraced,
and he pressed upon me a small black object, wizened
and of indeterminate shape. I examined it, but could make
nothing of it. I showed it to the others, who shook their
heads.

Suddenly, Wish gave a great cry and snatched the thing
out of my hand. It was a warple! A toasted and blackened
warple; but still a warple!

Wish asked Constant to find out about it. Pong told him
that the warple was considered a delicacy by the Yogistani.
His kitchen hands gathered them every morning before
breakfast.

Wish told Constant to offer *bohee* one for every warple
brought to him. The porters immediately scattered in all
directions, and soon started coming back with warples many,
which they dropped at Wish's feet after receiving their
money. Soon he had a pile some three feet high and was
bankrupt. He appealed to Constant to stop them; but they
went on until the district was denuded of warples. Wish was
now surrounded by a wall of warples and heavily in debt to
the expedition.

The porters were now ready to depart. Being a punctilious
race, they found it necessary to say good-bye all over again.
Once more the glacier rang with belches. Once more Pong
and I took an emotional farewell of each other. We little
dreamed that we should meet again before many months
were gone.

*

Next morning we made an early start. Wish had been up
all night making a distillation of warple exegesis, which he
carried in an exegesis bottle brought specially for the

purpose. Burley had kindly stayed up to help him. Wish was overjoyed. His presence on the expedition had been justified, his fame assured. He was, he said, almost certain of an FRS.

Shute took the lead. He too had been up all night, helping Jungle to finish his map. Jungle had complained of fatigue in the morning and had drunk the spirit out of his compasses. As a result he had become slightly tipsy and had developed a tendency to face north, which caused him to walk sideways when going east or west and fall over backwards when going south. Owing to the path twisting in all directions his movements became remarkable. Shute helped him good-naturedly, but Wish, who was following, became so bewildered that he went quite giddy and fell on his hip, smashing his exegesis bottle. The contents ran down his legs and froze, so that he was stiff-legged for the rest of the day and fell down frequently. Burley spent the day picking him up and consoling him for his bruises and the loss of the exegesis.

Constant and Prone followed. Being deprived of Pong's cooking, Constant had been awake all night with stomachache. Prone sat up with him, worrying himself to death over his friend's condition. Constant was also very down at losing his porters. To comfort him Prone walked with him, his arm around his shoulders. Unfortunately, they both fell into a crevasse, but were rescued by the porter.

I brought up the rear. I was quite sad when I turned my back on the majestic stage where we had played our drama of suffering and triumph. When my companions broke into song with 'Binder's Butter Beans' I almost sobbed. But I comforted myself with the thought that our suffering was not yet over; and as I followed the happy and united party I was cheered by the reflection that our friendship had been tempered into bonds of steel by the perils we had faced together. I was tasting the keener rewards of leadership.

*

Three days later we stood on the summit of the Rankling La, facing the Rum Doodle massif for the last time. The evening sun had sunk below our horizon. The wilderness of mountains around us was a symphony in modulated shadow. Below was the utter blackness of river gorges. Only Rum Doodle itself stood in the sunshine, its great pyramid framed against a turquoise sky. The vast icy precipices and snow-fields glowed with changing sunset tints.

It was a fitting farewell from a mighty mountain. Burley put his hand on my shoulder, and together we made our way through gathering darkness to our halting-place in the valley.

THE CRUISE
OF THE
TALKING FISH

To John, June, Magda, etc.

CONTENTS

CONTENTS
continued

'The sort of man who would
let a family of lizards live in his teapot' (page 12)

1   *'What on Earth are we Doing?'*

Away in the east the last headland slips under the horizon, and dry land becomes a memory. The world contracts to a circle of water, with the *Talking Fish* as its centre and a population of five half-naked men, two cats, one frog, an oyster and twenty-eight tins of sardines. We are alone at last with the sea and the sky and our great friend the sun, which pours its wealth upon us generously and unremittingly, browning our bodies and mellowing our philosophies.

Willy, flat on his back, stretches his arms luxuriously. 'I'm almost convinced,' he says, 'that sun-worship is the only true faith.'

'You're getting soft,' says Hugo, chewing a splinter of teak. He turns over on to his stomach and looks between the logs at the jumping, chuckling water.

Cwmlad Jones, who is wearing a leek in his swimming-trunks in honour of St. David's day, shakes his head doubtfully. 'Wonderful it is,' he agrees; 'but idolatry is something else altogether.'

It is Hugo's turn to shake his head. He shakes it. 'Gloh!' he cries, and we look at him curiously. His beard is caught between two logs and he has lost interest in the discussion.

'There you go again,' says Cwmlad Jones, 'you and your beard. I wonder you put up with it, mun.'

'Blb-blb-blb Nnnnngh!' says Hugo, and comes free with a jerk.

'Safer it would be for all of us,' says Cwmlad Jones, 'if you should remove it.'

9

'There's a shark at my toes,' says Batters, from below.

'Well done, old chap,' says Hugo.

I jot down the conversation in my notebook. An author's life is no sinecure, even on a raft in the Pacific.

My name is Binder. I am an author, on a raft in the Pacific. My life is no sinecure.

The smooth Pacific swell pulsates lazily, like the slow heartbeat of a sleeping world. The raft rises and falls like a cradle, lulling us to a waking dream. Sun-strong reality dissolves to fantasy. The present becomes timeless and incomprehensible. What on earth, we wonder, are we doing here?

Willy raises his head. 'What on earth are we doing here?' he asks.

Cwmlad Jones scratches his plump thigh — the left one. 'Something about fish, isn't it?'

'Who cares?' says Hugo sleepily, and we drift away on our private dreams.

It is necessary to account for our presence on a raft in the Pacific. For me, it all started with an unexpected letter from Willy Wagstaff, whom I had not met since our schooldays, inviting me to visit him at his flat. He hinted at an adventure after my own heart and said he knew I would not fail him.

I consulted my dear wife, who agreed that I could not fail an old schoolmate; and a dismal November evening found me knocking at the shabby door of an attic room in a depressing house in Tooting.

As I remembered him, Willy Wagstaff was a bony, spectacled and pale-faced boy with long untidy hair and a passion for natural history. He was good at examinations and bad at games, but was respected for an ability to release important smells from deceptively innocent chemicals.

The door of the attic was opened by a bony, spectacled and pale-faced man with long untidy hair and a frog in his hand. Framed certificates hung behind him and a broken golf club stood against the wall. On the table was a beaker containing some deceptively innocent chemicals, from which came an important smell.

We shook hands cordially, frightening the frog, who protested at the top of his voice. To my surprise Willy answered him in the same language. 'This is Darwin,' he said. 'He's spending the winter with me. He says he's glad to see you.'

This struck me as rather irregular; but not wishing

to hurt anybody's feelings I nodded to Darwin and re-marked that any friend of Willy's was a friend of mine.

'In that case,' said Willy, 'you have a lot of friends. Come in and meet them.'

The small room contained few of the usual necessities of life, but it was stocked from floor to ceiling with little creatures of every conceivable kind. They hopped about in cages and boxes, crawled all over the walls and peeped at me from underneath every chair and table. Their cheeping and squeaking was not unpleasant to the ear; but their effect on the nose, combined with that of the deceptively innocent chemicals, was something beyond my experience.

Willy shooed a pair of hedgehogs, whom he introduced as Hengist and Horsa, from a dilapidated armchair, and invited me to sit down. Reflecting that this would not commit me to any specific course of action, I did so. A field-mouse on the mantelpiece interrupted her toilet to nod to me. Her name was Cleopatra.

Willy had removed a family of lizards — the Starchers — from a teapot, and was brewing something. I had summed him up at a glance. He was the eager boffin type: a real enthusiast; good at his job, but apt to let enthusiasm get the better of judgment — the sort of man who would let a family of lizards live in his teapot.

'I hope you like seaweed tea,' he said. 'It's good for wrinkled kneecaps.' He took an oyster out of the milk-jug and put it in a bowl of salad. 'This is Neptune. He's having a pearl. He finds milk good for his complexion. If you take sugar, be careful of the ants. They're having a picnic.'

I sat on the edge of my chair, fending off a too-friendly turtle called Tannhäuser, who was having a nibble at my trousers; and listened to Willy's story.

Briefly, he was the victim of professional jealousy. In spite of a first-class brain and an unrivalled knowledge of natural history his opinions were disregarded. For years he had struggled against neglect, and had almost despaired of getting a hearing. Briefly, he was ignored.

A magpie called Margaret had settled on my right shoulder and was making a thorough nuisance of herself. Preoccupied as I was with Tannhäuser, I was quite unable to cope with Margaret. Briefly, I was having my ear chewed.

But that, said Willy, wasn't important. He was, he said, at last within sight of success. His theory, which constituted the most revolutionary advance in the history of revolutionary advances, had lacked only the proof of factual evidence. That evidence was now available; all he had to do was collect it.

All I had to do was grasp Tannhäuser firmly with my left hand and Margaret with my right. I did it; and a grass-snake called Gregory began to wriggle up my leg.

Willy said that an animal-lover like myself would have no difficulty in understanding his revolutionary theory, which was, briefly, that animals possess intelligence.

Crossing my legs to block the advance of Gregory, I said I didn't doubt it. Willy looked hurt.

'Not, of course,' I added tactfully, 'human intelligence.' I pressed my chin against my collar to keep out a snail called Stanley.

Willy was pleased. 'You're too conservative,' he told me. 'My theory is that animals are every bit as intelligent as human beings.'

I banged my left ear against my shoulder to dislodge an intelligent earwig named Ernest.

'No use shaking your head,' said Willy. 'I can prove it.'

Something called Simon was crawling down the back of my neck. I slid down in my chair and pressed the back of my neck against it.

The problem, Willy was saying, was one of communication. He had to find a creature he could talk to. Consulting the memoirs of celebrated animal-lovers, he had discovered that the seal could be trained to understand thirty-five words, against the dog's twelve. Willy deduced from this that sea-intelligence was higher than land-intelligence; and experiment confirmed this. The average oyster, he found, could distinguish eighty-eight words; while Neptune, a most intelligent creature, was responsive to no less than one hundred and nine.

'What about Darwin?' I asked.

'He doesn't count,' said Willy. 'He's a land animal.'

But, he went on, although these creatures could understand words, they could not speak them. The vocal chords of the oyster were rudimentary, and even Neptune seemed unable to master the Morse code. Willy had had to look elsewhere.

An owl called Oliver was trying to settle on my foot. As quickly as I kicked it away it would return.

The fish, said Willy, was the obvious choice, for he was man's ancestor. Recent developments in underwater swimming had revealed that the fish is affectionate and responsive to sound. Willy set himself the task of finding a species of fish capable both of understanding and reproducing human speech : briefly, a talking fish.

Willy asked me if I thought this a reasonable proposition. I said that, as he put it, it was one of the most reasonable propositions I had ever listened to. I told him I was anxious to hear the end of it.

His researches, he told me, took him to every corner of the ocean. He recorded interviews with fish of all kinds, and tried to persuade them to include language courses in their schools. He spent a fortune on waterproof exercise-books.

All to no purpose. After years of devoted work he returned home bankrupt, with nothing to show for his trouble.

He showed me some photographs.

'What are they?' I asked.

'Buburups,'' he explained.

'Really!' I said.

Buburups, he told me, were inhabitants of a small island in the middle of the Pacific. Willy had spent some weeks there recovering from a bout of wrinkled kneecaps caused by prolonged immersion in warm water. Unable to pursue his work, he had amused himself by study-ing the Buburup language, little thinking that those few amusing weeks were to prove more fruitful than years of devoted work.

'Does anything strike you about these people?' he asked.

'Yes,' I said. 'They have no clothes on.'

'No, no,' he said. 'Their fingers.'

'They haven't any.'

'Exactly!'

'I see your point,' I said.

'Now,' said Willy, 'I'm going to play you a recording of their language.' He removed an eagle's nest from his tape-recorder and set it in motion. 'What does it sound like?' he asked.

'Water coming out of a bottle,' I suggested.

'Exactly! Now listen carefully to the last bit.'

I listened carefully.

Willy switched off. 'What were they saying?' he asked.

'It sounded like "blum-blum",' I said.

'You have a good ear,' said Willy.

'Not at all,' I said. A baby alligator called Algy was climbing on to my knee and I was in no mood for compliments.

'Now,' said Willy, changing spools; 'I want you to listen to another record.'

It sounded to me exactly like the last portion of the first record: a chorus of voices saying 'blum-blum' over and over again. Then it became incoherent, and Willy switched off.

'You heard it?' he asked. He seemed excited. He had drawn a handkerchief out of his pocket and was wiping his forehead with Darwin.

'Yes,' I said. ' "Blum-blum", again.' Algy was nibbling my nose.

Willy apologised to Darwin and put him in the salad-bowl. He jumped on top of Neptune, who opened suddenly, throwing Darwin head-over-heels. The latter raised an indignant croak.

'Stop it, you two!' said Willy. 'That's no way to behave in company.'

Neptune blushed.

'They're showing off,' said Willy. 'They're usually quite well-behaved.'

'I'm sure they are,' I said.

'Well now,' he said. 'The word "blum-blum" is the Buburup word of greeting; it means both hello and good-bye. The first recording was their farewell to me when I left the island. The second recording . . . . You'll never guess what that was!'

I shook my head, dislodging a duck called Dan.

Willy leaned forward. 'It was an underwater recording of sounds made by fish!'

'No!' I cried. I was getting anxious about my nose. Choosing the lesser of two evils, I released Tannhäuser and grasped Algy, leaving my trousers to look after themselves. Stanley and Ernest were still trying to get at me and Margaret was struggling frantically to free herself. Gregory was having things all his own way.

'Are those creatures bothering you?' Willy asked.

'No, no,' I said.

'You have a true feeling for animals,' he told me. 'They seem to understand you perfectly.'

The second record, it appeared, had been made on a trans-Pacific raft voyage by a friend of Willy's who had allowed him to copy it. It proved conclusively that Buburup was the native language of a certain species of fish. Moreover, said Willy, it was clear that the Buburups must be direct descendents of these fish. Their language proved it, and the absence of fingers confirmed it. Fishes, also, he pointed out, have no fingers.

This was undeniable. I began to have a new respect for Willy. 'What are you going to do about it?' I asked.

The thing to do, he said, was to find the talking fish. Unfortunately, his friend had got his spools mixed up and didn't know within a thousand miles or so where the recording had been made. Willy intended to duplicate the conditions of his friend's voyage exactly, by setting out on a raft from the same place on the same day, making recordings at frequent intervals.

'But why,' I asked, 'are you telling me all this?'

'I want you to come along.'

'It's a great honour,' I said; 'but I really couldn't. I'm a family man, you know.'

'It's only for three months,' said Willy.

Things were reaching a climax. Algy had broken loose and was attacking my lower lip. Tannhäuser had eaten my left trouser leg as far as the knee. Reinforcements were pouring in from all directions. Something, I decided, had to be done, and done quickly.

'But why me?' I asked. 'Surely there are others.'

'Nobody,' said Willy, 'with your qualifications.'

'True,' I agreed. I was in a quandary. A woodpecker called Wilfred had settled on my nose and was examining my forehead. Should I release Margaret? An immediate decision was essential.

'Would you stamp my insurance cards?' I asked.

'Every day,' said Willy.

'I'll come!' I said. 'Now get me out of this.'

At my suggestion our next meeting took place at my flat. I said that too many visits to Willy's room might over-excite his friends. He brought Darwin and Neptune with him — they both enjoyed a tube journey — and asked if he might borrow a bowl of milk.

Darwin croaked twice.

'Pasteurised,' said Willy.

The two animals were put into the bowl, and immediately started to splash each other. Willy said that if they didn't behave he would have to put them in his pocket. Darwin croaked indignantly. 'I don't care who started it,' said Willy. 'You're a later stage of evolution and should make allowances.'

Darwin hung his head sulkily; and Neptune began to quiver.

'I presume,' I said, 'that you want me to get a crew together?'

'Well,' said Willy, 'not exactly. As a matter of fact, I've chosen them already.'

'Oh,' I said. 'But you want me to lead the expedition, naturally?'

'Not exactly,' said Willy. 'As a matter of fact, I was going to lead it myself.'

'I see,' I said. 'You'd like me to be responsible for the nautical arrangements.'

'Not precisely,' said Willy. 'As a matter of fact, I've asked Hugo Hurlstrom to do that.'

'After all,' I said, 'the commissariat is the most important part of an expedition.'

'As a matter of fact,' said Willy, 'Cwmlad Jones will be in charge of it.'

'You seem to have it all worked out,' I said. 'As a matter of fact.'

'As a matter of fact,' said Willy, 'I have.'

'And these two — er — gentlemen: who are they?'

'I've invited them here today,' said Willy. 'I hope you don't mind?'

'Not at all,' I said. 'Why should I?'

'That's probably one of them now,' said Willy.

The new arrival was a large newcomer whom I summed up at a glance as a man to be wary of. He was tall and strongly built, and carried himself like one in perfect physical shape. His hair was red and his face weatherbeaten. His hands were exceptionally large and heavy. He was, I knew at once, completely devoid of a sense of humour.

His first words confirmed my diagnosis. 'Menagerie ahoy!' he cried, in a terribly hearty voice. 'I see we have a new specimen. What is it — fish, fowl or insect?'

'This is Hugo Hurlstrom,' said Willy. 'I've asked him to be responsible for the nautical arrangements.'

'And this,' said the large newcomer, 'will be the famous Binder.'

He seized my hand, and gripped it so tightly that I had difficulty in stifling a cry of distress.

'What was that?' said Hurlstrom.

'Nothing,' I said. 'Just a twinge of liver.'

'Look after it, old boy,' he said. 'Life depends on the liver!' He roared with laughter.

'How's the livestock today?' he said. 'The pearl seems to be coming along nicely.' He poked his finger inside Neptune, who closed with a snap, giving him a nasty nip.

Darwin leaped on top of his friend and jumped up and down, croaking loudly. Willy winked at him and put a finger to his lips.

Hurlstrom, he told me, was the most experienced rafts-man alive. He had crossed the Atlantic on a dining-room table.

'With the leaf missing,' said Hurlstrom, sucking his finger.

'His sufferings,' said Willy, 'broke three world records.'

'Can't expect anything sensational on a picnic like this,' said Hurlstrom. 'But we might do something interesting with a monotonous diet — putty and sawdust, perhaps.'

'I have a weak stomach,' I said, somewhat alarmed.

'Lucky chap!' said Hurlstrom. 'You're half-way there already. Not an ulcer, by any chance?'

'No,' I said.

'Try vinegar. That sometimes works wonders.'

'I'll consider it,' I said.

At that moment the doorbell rang again, and my wife brought in a round, chubby little man not much taller than myself. Willy introduced him as Cwmlad Jones, who would be in charge of the commissariat.

'You will be the famous Binder, then,' said Cwmlad Jones, in a soft and musical voice. 'Your adventures are well-known to all. I hope it hasn't gone to your head.'

Although I am accustomed to sum a man up at a glance, there was something about this Welshman that I found disconcerting. I felt that I lacked the clue to his personality, and decided that I had better deal warily with him until I knew where we stood. I remarked civilly that I hoped I had retained my humility.

'A rare thing, indeed,' said Cwmlad Jones, and turned to the animals. Neptune had opened at the sound of his voice and was making a great display of his pearl. 'Coming along nicely, it is,' said Cwmlad Jones. 'There's pretty you are, mun.'

Neptune blushed.

'But it's vain you are too, you silly creature.'

Darwin croaked impatiently.

'Jealous, is it?' said Cwmlad Jones, patting the frog's head. 'Never mind, mun; I'll sing you a song, after.'

Darwin jumped with pleasure, spilling the milk.

'If you are behaving yourself,' added Cwmlad Jones.

Willy explained that Cwmlad Jones — or C.J., as they called him — had been advised by a specialist to take some suffering for the good of his soul. 'We call him C.J.,' he added.

'I understand perfectly,' I said, somewhat disturbed by this talk of suffering. 'But I'm not clear about my own job.'

'It's all a question of negotiation,' said Willy. 'We didn't want to decide in your absence.'

'Very thoughtful of you,' I said gratefully.

'It depends on the requirements of the expedition, of course.'

'Of course,' I said. 'What are they?'

'Well,' said Willy; 'you'll understand that an expedition of this kind costs money.'

'Naturally,' I said.

'A lot of money.'

'I'm sure it does,' I said.

'How much?' I said.

'Five thousand pounds.'

'Hm!' I said.

'It's like this, old boy,' said Hurlstrom. 'Nobody can ever afford a raft expedition. They're far too expensive.'

'I see your point,' I said.

'Beforehand,' he added.

'Eh?' I said.

Hurlstrom explained. 'You borrow the money, and write a book about your sufferings to pay it back.'

'I see,' I said.

'It's quite simple.'

'It seems to be. Does it always work?'

'Invariably.'

'I'm glad to hear it.' I said. 'I see now what you want me for: you want me to find somebody to lend us the money.'

'More or less,' said Willy.

I was thinking rapidly. 'Look here,' I said. 'How would it be if I were to advance the money myself?'

'By jove!' said Willy. 'What a good idea!'

'Why didn't we think of it?' said Hurlstrom.

'Slipping, we are,' said C.J.

'Is that agreed, then?' I asked.

'Agreed!' agreed everybody.

There is — or should be — a moment in all expeditions when the members cease to be individuals and become parts of a whole. It is at this moment that the experienced campaigner relaxes for the first time, knowing that whatever hardships and dangers lie ahead there is not one of his companions who will not offer his utmost in the common cause. It is at this moment that he sees his fellow-members in a new way, and sighs as he reaches some subtle psychological haven.

This was such a moment. Ceasing to be an individual, I saw my fellow-members in a new way. Willy, I saw, was the perfect leader: not too cautious, not too sensitive, not too modest. Hugo was a tower of strength — a little deficient in humour, perhaps, but lovable for that very human failing. How absurd it was that I had thought it necessary to be wary of him. And C.J. — how foolish it had been to mistrust his depth of character, which must surely be an enrichment to all of us. And how ridiculous it was to have suspected Darwin of selfishness in his relationship with Neptune.

Overcome by the significance of the occasion, I pressed the hands of my companions. He is a blessed man who knows this moment of union. He is a twice-blessed man who knows it twice. He is a thrice-blessed man who knows it three times.

It was too much. I turned away to hide a tear.

'Who will write the book?' I asked, recovering.

'We thought you would like to do it,' said Willy.

On a morning in early February we touched down at the Equatorio airfield and drove in tropical sunshine to the Deep Sea Sufferers' Club, where we were welcomed by the Secretary, Truleigh Travelworn, an emaciated person of indeterminate age wearing a canvas shirt and horse-hair trousers.

'You're looking well,' he told Hugo, disapprovingly. 'Hope you're not getting soft, old man.'

'It's this damned constitution of mine,' Hugo explained, and introduced us. 'This is the famous Binder,' he concluded. 'He has a weak stomach.'

'Lucky chap!' said Travelworn. 'Not an ulcer, I suppose?'

'No,' I said, apologetically.

'Come and have a cocktail,' said Travelworn, and led us to a corrugated-iron lean-to. 'What'll it be?'

'Could I have a lemonade?' I asked.

Travelworn roared with laughter. 'That's a good one!' he cried, dealing me a severe blow beween the shoulder-blades. 'Did you hear that, Hurlstrom? A glass of lemonade! Damned funny! Make it gin-and-sulphuric, bartender.'

'Lemonade!' he chuckled, wiping his eyes.

'So you're taking the Gumbolt current,' he remarked, when drinks had been handed round. 'Bit of a come-down, old boy, isn't it?'

'I'm just filling in time,' said Hugo.

'I should hope so. How will you make it interesting?'

'I had thought of putty and sawdust.'

'You couldn't do better. We make some splendid putty here: no nourishment value whatsoever.'

'I'll take half a ton,' said Hugo.

'You won't regret it,' said Travelworn. 'Did you bring your own sawdust?'

'No.'

'You were wise. The English stuff just isn't bad enough. Too well sawn, for one thing. With your reputation you can't afford to take chances. I can get you some excellent teak.'

'With splinters?'

'Regulation pattern. Certificate goes with it.'

'I'll take fifteen hundredweight,' said Hugo. 'What sort of a season has it been?'

'Quiet. Chiefly beginners. The old hands make for the Antarctic, nowadays. You'll be building your own raft, of course?'

'My dear chap!'

'Sorry, old boy,' said the Secretary. 'It's these beginners; they buy them second-hand from each other. One forgets.' He looked in all directions, and lowered his voice to a whisper. 'You mustn't let it go any further, old boy; but I caught one bounder trying to hire one from a native.'

'Good God!' said Hugo.

'It shows you, doesn't it?'

Hugo drained his glass. 'Fill 'em up again, bartender!'

Willy and I exchanged worried glances. I signalled with my eyes and poured my drink into a flower-pot which contained a healthy-looking orchid. Willy managed to reach behind me and do the same. C.J. put his glass on the bar. His drink was untouched. 'No more for me,' he said firmly. 'Better I am without it.'

Travelworn was a study in raised eyebrows. He lifted his glass to Hugo. 'Here's wishing you a rotten journey!'

'Thanks, old man,' said Hugo. 'Can you help me with the materials?'

'Feller you want is Batters. Knows the jungle backwards. There he is now. Batters, old boy!'

Batters was a stocky person of indeterminate age who seemed to have been carved out of limestone. He wore an emery-cloth shirt and linoleum shorts, and was smoking a pipe of the vilest-smelling mixture I had ever encountered. Travelworn introduced us, finishing with myself. 'This is the famous Binder,' he said. 'He has a weak stomach.'

'Ulcer?' said Batters.

I shook my head.

'Pity,' said Batters.

'Made a damned good joke, just now,' said Travelworn. 'Asked for a glass of lemonade. Damned funny, what?'

'Damned funny,' said Batters, without moving a muscle of his face.

'I knew you'd like it,' said Travelworn. 'Hurlstrom here wants to build a raft. Told him you could advise him.'

'Come to the right place,' said Batters.

'Just what I told him, old man.'

'Know the jungle backwards,' said Batters.

'I told you, didn't I?' said Travelworn. 'He knows the jungle backwards.'

'Nice it would be,' said C.J., 'if he knew it forwards.' Travelworn looked at him coldly. 'Let's discuss it over lunch,' he suggested. 'We're serving a very tough horse's hoof.'

Willy and I looked at each other apprehensively. 'I think,' he said, 'I'll do without lunch.'

Travelworn looked offended. 'My dear man,' he said; 'you're my guest.'

'I have my animals to attend to,' Willy explained.

'Ah!' said the Secretary. 'That's different.'

Willy glanced at me apologetically.

'I think,' I said desperately, 'that I'll do without lunch, too.'

'My dear fellow!' said the Secretary.

'A fast,' I explained. 'A little suffering, you know.'

'Ah!' said the Secretary. 'Say no more, old chap!'

'I am thinking,' said C.J., 'that horse's hoof is not a good thing for my stomach. At the hotel I will eat.'

'Good God!' said the Secretary.

As we left the lean-to I glanced at the orchid. It was not the flower it had been.

Two days later we went up-country to collect materials
for the raft. Batters had kindly offered his services, and
the first hundred miles were done in his jeep — a dilapidated vehicle which he had salvaged from a rubbish-dump.
We camped the first night on the bank of a wide river at
the edge of the jungle. Batters, who liked to live off the
country, went off with a huge elephant-gun to hunt for
our supper. Game was plentiful, and we licked our lips
in anticipation. When several startling explosions were
heard we nodded to each other approvingly.

It was midnight when Batters returned. The barrel of
his gun was red-hot and he had burnt his hands badly.
His kill was slung over his shoulder; it was a thin animal
the size of a kitten.

'Never known game so scarce,' he said. 'We'll have to
ration ourselves.'

Hugo nodded approvingly.

The animal was roasted over the camp-fire — all except
the skin, which Batters cut into strips to be dried and used
as emergency ration. During supper we were badly bitten
by swarms of insects; and afterwards, Batters, who liked
to smoke off the country, filled his pipe with under-
growth and puffed up a dense and most revolting cloud
of smoke. He discussed with Hugo our prospects of
suffering, and said he was optimistic.

Next day we moved off at dawn, after breakfasting on
emergency ration. Batters went first, carrying an enormous load; and behind him was Hugo, similarly laden.

The rest of us carried nothing but our personal gear: a pair of pyjamas and a detective story. Willy brought up the rear. He was sad and a little lonely; Darwin and Neptune had had to be left in quarantine, and he missed them. He was worried, too, about his other friends, left behind in the attic. He had arranged a balance of life for them, so that none need go hungry; but he tortured himself with thoughts of what might happen if the balance should be upset.

The trail was a narrow tunnel with walls of impenetrable vegetation, roofed over by branches and creepers. When we reached a cross-roads Batters chose his way unhesitatingly. Shortly after setting off he had stumbled, gashing his leg badly on a broken bamboo stem. Without breaking his stride he bound up the wound with a dirty rag and plunged onwards. Hugo murmured a word of congratulation.

At noon Batters announced tiffin, and handed round the last scraps of emergency ration. Hugo refused his share, saying he would cut himself some bark. While he was doing so the knife slipped and he slashed his hand. 'Lend me a bit of dirty rag, old boy,' he said, and wrapped it loosely round his hand.

Batters nodded approvingly.

The rest of the day's trek was a nightmare. Batters smoked incessantly, and the fumes from his terrible pipe hung heavy in the tunnel, choking the rest of us who had to pass through them. It was with great relief that we came at last to a break in the jungle and saw the evening sun setting over a wide river.

A dilapidated jeep was standing on the bank.

We were back at our starting-point.

Batters came back from his hunt with a skinny bird

the size of a pigeon. 'Plenty of suffering here,' he said. He stripped off the emergency ration and flung the remainder to Hugo. 'Look after this, old man. I'm going to have a bout of jungle fever.'

'How do you do it?' said Hugo admiringly.

The next day's march was even more harrowing than the first. Batters' leg had begun to fester, and he was in high spirits; but Hugo, whose hand was healing, was morose and touchy. The rest of us had jettisoned our pyjamas, but it was as much as we could do to maintain the pace set by the heavily-laden Batters.

After a lunch of emergency ration, which was mainly feathers, we entered a swamp, and waded for several miles waist-deep. Herds of alligators were kept at bay by Batters; but nothing could discourage the clouds of insects, which attacked every part of our exposed skin, or the leeches, which penetrated our clothing and did dreadful things to the remaining areas.

It was with infinite relief that we emerged at last from the swamp, to fling ourselves down, weak and hungry, in the shade of the jeep.

After supper, which consisted of a bony creature the size of a rat, C.J. drew Willy and myself aside and said it was enough he had had. He had, he said, no intention of tramping the jungle until he was nothing but skin and grief. He suggested a mutiny.

Saddened, I reminded him that we were not individuals, but members of an expedition; it was our duty to offer our utmost in the common cause. C.J. replied that the common cause was to find the talking fish, not to provide suffering for Hugo and his demented friends. I reminded him that he himself had come in search of suffering for the good of his soul; but he said that his soul had

had all the suffering it could stand; what it wanted from now on was a life of ease with three square meals a day. This, he said, was a spiritual necessity; his conscience insisted on it.

I said I could not advise a man against his own conscience, but suggested that he might sleep on it; which he agreed to do. I retired for the night in no enviable state of mind. Before dropping off I heard Hugo asking Batters what he had got lined up for tomorrow. 'It's the mountain course,' said the latter. 'You get some interesting high-altitude effects.'

I spent a wretched night, haunted by nightmares of Hugo and Batters at high altitudes. In the morning I felt quite below par and unable to face the emergency ration. C.J. took my pulse and said I was suffering from justifiable nausea. It was essential, he said, that I should rest for several days. He offered to nurse me. Willy said it was noble of him, and offered to help.

Batters and Hugo were very decent about it. They said they could get along quite well by themselves. They said I wasn't to worry about them. They marched off like two schoolboys on a holiday adventure, Batters, whose leg was much worse, leaning heavily on his friend.

I watched them go with mixed feelings. If they should perish, I thought, I would never forgive myself for not having died with them.

I asked C.J. how he came to know about justifiable nausea. He said that an uncle of his had died of it during an election. I said I supposed I had better lie down and rest. He said that gentle exercise was what I needed, and suggested that I might look after the camp-fire and do the cooking.

He and Willy went off hunting. The game proved to

be quite tame if not frightened by loud noises; it allowed itself to be caught in the friendliest way. We ate our fill and slept ourselves out, and had a delightful swim in the river.

Towards evening the travellers returned. Hugo had broken his leg on the mountain and had been carried back by Batters, whose own leg was now a dreadful sight. They had had nothing to eat all day and could not conceal their delight. Hugo's first action, when thrown on the ground, was to take out his sufferer's mirror and examine his face for emaciation. Batters went off on his hunt, and returned empty-handed; and I thought for a moment that Hugo was going to faint with joy.

We spent eight days by the river. Every morning Batters and Hugo staggered off on another ordeal; and every evening they returned, dined off some minute creature and compared sufferings. Hugo's leg had been put in splints; an improvised crutch enabled him to hobble about quite actively. Batters' leg had to be seen to be believed.

On the ninth day Batters said that the jungle course was complete; work could begin on the raft.

The art of raft-making is an established tradition among the deep-sea suffering fraternity. The timber used is that of the *basta* tree, which is chosen for its property of growing only in the impenetrable jungle. The early pioneers had taken their trees from the most inaccessible part of the jungle, which was ten days' safari from the most accessible part. When all the *basta* trees in this area had been cut down it was agreed that the more accessible trees might be taken, provided that a ten-day safari was completed. Suitable courses were laid out and strict rules made; and it was generally agreed that, if anything, the safaris to the more accessible parts were even stiffer than those to the inaccessible ones.

Under Batters' direction we set about the felling of ten tall trees in the impenetrable jungle. The first problem was to penetrate the jungle and find the trees. The next was to fell them. The last was to get them out of the jungle. Having done this, we stripped them of boughs and cut the trunks into logs of suitable length, which were rolled into the river. Logs of suitable length were then cut from the boughs, and these were also rolled into the river. The first lot of logs were now some distance down-stream, and had to be brought back. While we were bringing them back the second lot drifted past on the other side of the river, and we had to abandon the first lot to retrieve them. While we were retrieving them the first lot floated past.

Batters said he couldn't understand it; it had never happened before. He could only conclude that river conditions must be different from what they were at other building-sites. He said he didn't see any solution; we must abandon the logs and start all over again.

This time the materials were assembled on the bank; logs and creepers, poles, and reeds for matting. We sat down to consider what was to be done next. Batters made experiments with models, and said the thing was hopeless; there was no way of preventing the material floating away before the raft was constructed.

C.J. said it was a pity he hadn't made his experiments earlier.

Hugo suggested trying again further upstream; but Batters said there were no trees left there. This building-site, he said, was the only possible one. As far as he could see, it meant the end of rafting in this part of the world.

It was Willy's scientific brain which found a solution. 'Why don't we build it on the bank?' he asked.

Batters looked at him coldly. 'I was just going to suggest it,' he said.

So we built our raft by the side of the river — under the direction of Hugo, who said that this was where he took over. We lashed the large logs together with creepers, put the small ones on top of them, and covered the whole with matting. A matting-covered cabin was built, and a matting sail was hoisted. It was a trim little craft.

But when we tried to push it into the water it wouldn't go. It was far too heavy.

Batters said he knew it all the time; it was the end of rafting in this part of the world.

Willy had another idea. We should dismantle the raft, launch the materials and let them float downstream. We would drive down to the river-mouth and intercept the materials when they got there.

Batters said it had been on the tip of his tongue. He was, he said, sick of being interrupted.

So we dismantled the raft, launched the materials and watched them float downstream. We packed our belongings in the jeep and climbed aboard.

The jeep refused to start.

Batters investigated; he had run out of petrol. He said he had known from the beginning the thing was hopeless. He said it was a damned silly expedition anyway; it served him right for having anything to do with it.

'It's a very good expedition,' said Willy indignantly. 'And it isn't hopeless. We don't need your rotten jeep; we can walk.'

'Suffering we can have,' said C.J.

'By Jove!' said Batters, his eyes lighting up. 'I knew we'd make out! Never say die: that's my motto!'

Willy made a calculation and decided that we had eight days to cover the hundred miles. We set off at once, pushing the jeep, which Batters refused to leave behind. C.J. steered.

It was an eventful journey. On the first day we were attacked by bandits and robbed of our clothing. On the second day we contracted sunburn in unusual places and had to stop to hunt for fig trees. On the third day Batters discovered that we were walking in the wrong direction. On the fourth day our sufferings became indescribable.

On the ninth day we reached Equatorio and were cheered through the streets. The timber, we were told, had passed through the previous day and was now dotted about the bay. Batters and Hugo swam out to retrieve it, and underwent such suffering that they were officially congratulated by the committee of the Sufferers' Club, who had watched the whole thing from the quay. Batters said perhaps it wasn't such a bad expedition, after all.

We lost no time in rebuilding the raft, and soon the stores were being loaded under C.J.'s supervision. He had flatly refused to consider a putty-and-sawdust diet, and after much discussion it was agreed that Hugo might follow it if he liked; the rest of us would take normal food. Hugo sold three-quarters of his order back to Travelworn, at considerable financial loss to me.

Darwin and Neptune had been installed on board in a bowl of condensed milk. Darwin seemed overjoyed to be with us, and Neptune's pearl was coming along nicely. Hugo had acquired two cats; he said they would keep the rats down. They were ginger cats; their names were Plato and Aristotle.

Willy had asked me to sign a statement accepting complete financial responsibility for the expedition. He pointed out that I was actually already responsible, since I was going to finance the expedition out of my royalties. He said that the signature was just a formality as far as I was concerned, but it would enable him to put his own affairs in order. I was glad to do as he asked.

Just before we sailed, Hugo asked if anybody knew where Batters was; and we realised that he had not been seen for two days. After the town had been searched he was found hanging from the lower logs of the raft, his head above and his body in the water. His neck had evidently been caught between two logs during the building. His face was purple, with yellow spots, and his tongue protruded. He was unconscious.

We made a hole in the flooring above him and sat around it, considering what we should do. I was for releasing him; but Hugo said that he was in an excellent suffering position and we had no right to interfere. 'Better loosen the logs, though,' he said. 'He can't suffer while he's unconscious.'

This was done, and Batters soon came round. When he realised his position he was delighted, and begged us to take him with us. I was not too happy about the expense; but Hugo said we owed it to Batters after all he had done for us. So we signed him on as a member of the crew, and Hugo hurried to the Club for more putty and sawdust — which, he found, had risen sharply in price.

Our departure was made the occasion of a public holiday, and a tremendous crowd turned out to see us off. The wife of the mayor of Equatorio, a most attractive young woman of the tropical type, had kindly consented to perform the naming ceremony. 'I name this raft *Talking Fish*,' she said. 'Heaven help all who sail on her.' She smashed a magnum of nitric acid on the deck, and had started to kiss us all round when her husband fortunately intervened.

Travelworn came aboard at the last moment, to wish us a miserable voyage and put official seals on the creepers which held Batters in position. Then Hugo dived into the water with a rope round his waist to tow us into the Gumbolt current. The whole population of Equatorio cheered as we moved out slowly on our great adventure.

We have now been a week at sea, and are shaking down well to the raftsman's life. All are in good health, except for Batters, who has a pain in the neck. Plato and Aristotle are shaking down as though they had never done anything else in their lives. Darwin shakes wonderfully well for such a small animal, and Neptune does the best he can; his pearl is coming along nicely.

We have established a daily routine which keeps us busy and cheerful. The day has been divided into four periods of six hours, which are shared between the two watches. The port watch, consisting of Hugo and Batters, takes the first and third periods, and the starboard watch the other two. This arrangement works well; in fact, since no particular duties are assigned to the watches it has no effect whatsoever on the daily routine. The starboard watch sleeps in the cabin, but the port watch scorns such luxury. We rise at eight o'clock — or eight bells, as we call it — and start the day by throwing overboard the flying fish which have landed on deck during the night. Then the starboard watch shaves while the port watch combs its beards and examines its faces for signs of suffering. Then breakfast is cooked and eaten. At my request a system of democratic government has been established, and I have been appointed cook of the starboard watch by majority vote. After breakfast we put on our apparatus and go below for some underwater swimming, leaving Batters to look after the raft. We make friends with the local fish and try to get them to talk. Willy makes tape-recordings of them, while C.J. tests them for radioactivity with a Geiger counter. We examine Batters' kneecaps for incipient wrinkling and take note of any barnacles which may have attached themselves to him during the night.

At noon we return to the raft and prepare lunch. Hugo makes an observation and works out our position, which usually turns out to be Omsk, or Birmingham, or some other impossible place. After lunch we rest for an hour, while I refill the aqualung air-cylinder with a hand-pump; this, by democratic vote, is my special responsibility. Neptune's milk is changed and the progress of the pearl is noted in the log. Following this, Willy gives us a lesson in spoken Buburup, in which we are becoming quite fluent, and we splice knots and furl the lee scuppers. At six bells C.J. switches on the short-wave radio receiver and tries to get the daily news bulletin which is specially transmitted to us from Equatorio. Power for the radio is supplied by a hand generator, turned democratically by myself. At seven we have our evening meal, after which we sit round Batters' hatch-coaming and yarn until ten bells, when we brew a cup of *Marvelcap,* sing a sea-shanty and retire for the night.

Batters' day, of course, is different. He spents his time suffering and smoking seaweed, which Hugo picks for him off the sea bottom. It produces the foulest smoke I have yet encountered.

Sometimes the routine is varied, for variety. Neptune, perhaps, is taken for an underwater picnic, or Darwin enlivens our evening with a display of acrobatics. He is on good terms with the cats; but they seem suspicious of Neptune, who snaps at them when they try to drink his milk. Willy says that evolution has provided them with no means of coping with oysters and they are having to make readjustments. The difference between Neptune open and Neptune closed seems to intrigue them. When he is in the closed position they creep round him in a circle, making tentative dabs with their paws. They are trying, Willy says, to invent a method of getting him open. They feed themselves on flying fish, which C.J. tests with the Geiger counter. This morning he found them eating a radioactive fish. He threw it overboard and tested the cats, finding both of them to be slightly radioactive. Willy says there may be some interesting consequences.

The inconsistencies in Hugo's calculations leave us in some doubt about our progress; but he has worked it out by dead reckoning, and reckons that we are making about a hundred miles a day, which, he says, is quite good going for the Gumbolt current.

We are a contented little crew; and although I sometimes sigh for my dear wife and look forward to the moment of reunion, I am happy to be here. I have just put into the sea a bottle containing a letter to my wife; it is nice to think that some years hence this message from the past may reach her. Will I be alive to share her joy? It is a solemn thought.

Today rather an odd thing happened. Hugo was aloft reefing the fore-tops'l halyards when he got his beard caught in a binnacle. Without thinking, he gave a cry of distress; and C.J., who was heaving ho, seized a pair of scissors and ran to free his friend. He was halfway up the mainmast when Hugo saw the scissors and realised his peril. He gave a hoarse cry and kicked C.J. overboard. The latter, who cannot swim, called for help, and Willy, crying 'Man overboard!', dived in after him. The two drifted quickly astern, and I saw that they were in danger of being left behind. I immediately threw out a lifebelt, which hit C.J. on the head, knocking him unconscious. Willy seized the lifebelt with one hand and C.J. with the other, and called to me to haul them in. As I bent to pick up the line I saw the end of it vanishing over the side. I made a grab for it and fell overboard myself.

A more desperate situation can hardly be imagined. A stiff breeze was driving the raft rapidly away. Hugo, swinging from the yardarm by his beard, could do nothing to help us. It seemed as if we should perish miserably, far from home and loved ones. It was not a happy thought. I imagined the *Talking Fish* drifting around the oceans of the world with one dead man hanging above and another below — becoming, perhaps, a grim sea legend like the Flying Dutchman, while the fate of the starboard watch became another unsolved mystery of the sea.

Short of a miraculous change of wind, I could see no possibility of rescue. I could not swim fast enough to overtake the raft; and land was a thousand miles away. I began to prepare for the end, and resolved that my last thoughts should be of my dear wife.

I was roused from my meditations by the sound of an engine. A trim motor-launch appeared beside my left ear. A face appeared over the side, saying: 'Is everything under control, old boy?'

It was Travelworn!

'What on earth are you doing here?' I asked.

'This is the Equatorio harbour-patrol,' he said. 'They let me come with them on my birthday.'

'Many happy returns,' I said. 'How old are you?'

'Forty-eight.'

'Really?' I said. 'You don't look a day over forty.'

'Nice of you to say so.'

'Not at all,' I said. 'But where are we?'

'Equatorio harbour, of course,' said Travelworn. 'Where did you think you were?'

I explained.

'Very interesting,' said Travelworn. 'Did you want to be rescued?'

'Yes please,' I said.

'Hm!' said Travelworn.

'I have an old father,' I explained.

I was hauled aboard — a painful process — and the other two were rescued, to Travelworn's great disgust. C.J. had recovered consciousness and was inclined to resent the whole thing.

The raft was overtaken and we climbed aboard. Willy went aloft to release Hugo; but the latter said he preferred to stay where he was; he said it was too good a chance to miss. Travelworn said he was glad that somebody had some spirit.

He said we must have drifted out of the Gumbolt current, and offered to tow us back into it. We accepted gratefully, and an hour later they waved us good-bye. Travelworn said we'd be glad to hear that a hurricane was expected.

The port watch being immobilised, arrangements had to be made for feeding them. This duty, by democratic vote, was assigned to me.

Plato and Aristotle are behaving very strangely. They do things at twice the usual speed, and have enormous appetites. Willy says that the radioactive fish must have affected their glands. They spend most of their leisure time trying to open Neptune.

This evening C.J. picked up the news that extensive manoeuvres by the combined allied fleets are to commence very shortly in the Pacific. I can only hope that they do not manoeuvre in our direction.

The last three days have been a nightmare. We have been drenched and battered by the full force of a tropical hurricane. Our sufferings are probably unique in the history of navigation. It is a miracle that we are still alive.

On the morning following our dramatic rescue we were preparing for our underwater swim when Willy remarked on a change in the weather. Dense and gloomy clouds were being driven across the sky by a tremendous wind, which whipped the sea to a cauldron of boiling foam and whined and howled in the rigging. The scene was bathed in an unearthly yellow light. Thunder rumbled in the distance.

C.J. said it looked like rain.

I was of the same opinion, and suggested that we might postpone our swim. We had just agreed to this when C.J. gave a strangled cry and pointed upwind. An enormous wave was bearing down on us. It must have been five hundred feet high and was travelling with the speed of an express train.

'Make fast the mizzen staysail!' cried Willy, springing to the roof of the cabin.

'No, no,' I said. 'Wear the starboard quarter.'

'Nonsense!' said Willy. 'Do as you're told.'

I reminded him that we were a democracy.

Willy said that this was no time for argument. I reminded him that our forefathers had bled for democracy; it was not to be relinquished at the first petty emergency.

'All right,' said Willy. 'We'll take a vote. All those in favour of me being captain say "Aye-aye, sir".'

'Aye-aye, sir,' said everybody, touching their foreheads. From the cabin came a croak from Darwin.

The wave was towering over us: an awe-inspiring sight.

'We'll try and outrun her,' said Willy. 'Put on more sail.'

'There isn't any more,' said C.J.

'Well, do something,' said Willy. 'Don't just stand there.'

At that moment a tremendous gust of wind burst on us, nearly driving us under water. The raft leaped forwards like a greyhound, gaining a few yards on the wave. The sail filled like a clap of thunder and began to tear.

'Lower the mainsail!' shouted Willy.

We sprang to the ropes and did so.

Hugo was now stretched out horizontally by the force of the wind, flying overhead like a pennant and spinning round on his beard. If the beard should give he would be blown away like a leaf. He said later that he hadn't been so happy since childhood.

But the strain was bending the mast like a fishing-rod. Suddenly, there was a loud crack.

'Lower Hugo!' cried Willy.

'We can't,' said C.J. 'He's a fixture.'

The raft was rolling and pitching in a mountainous sea. Rain was driving hard, blinding us with its needles. The raft was in danger of being blown to pieces. We clung for our lives to the gimbals.

A sudden gust almost tore the cabin away. 'Lower cabin!' cried Willy, and we sprang to obey. At that moment the mast gave way. 'Clew the fore top gallant spinnaker!' cried Willy.

'The *what*?' shouted C.J.

A flash of lightning struck the raft.

'Abandon bowsprit!' cried Willy.

The wave was upon us. 'Paint the figurehead!' cried Willy, and flung himself flat on the deck.

I have a confused recollection of being pressed down by tons of water and getting C.J.'s foot in my mouth. Ages passed, in which I thought of my dear wife and held my breath until my lungs were bursting. I remember reflecting that Batters must be having the time of his life.

The pressure eased, and C.J. removed his foot. I felt the wind on my face and drew in great gulps of air. I looked around me.

The *Talking Fish* was still afloat, intact except for the mast. The crew was all present and correct. Hugo had come loose from his binnacle and was swearing to himself in Buburup. Darwin and Neptune were huddled in a bowl of sea-water. The cats were doing things at five times normal speed.

The hurricane continued for three days. We had nothing to eat or drink and were worn out with work and lack of sleep. Neptune went down with sea-sickness, but was nursed devotedly by Darwin, who is inclined to be vain about his sea-legs. Batters, protected from the wind, was having the easiest time, and was inclined to be bitter about it.

On the morning of the fourth day the storm blew itself out. Apart from the loss of the mast we are none the worse for the ordeal; except perhaps for Hugo, who is still touchy about the suffering he has lost. There is much speculation about our position. Hugo has worked it out three times, getting New York, Boston and Chicago; but we feel fairly confident that we are still somewhere in the Pacific.

A very queer thing has happened. Aristotle has had kittens: six of them, all ginger. C.J. says the radioactive fish must have had something to do with it; but Willy thinks it happened in the usual way; Aristotle, he says, must have been a lady cat all the time.

Darwin doesn't understand it at all. Willy has tried to explain it to him, but he says that Darwin just doesn't seem to know the facts of life. Willy thinks he has been misled by Neptune's pearl.

While we were discussing it I heard Batters ask Hugo, in a stage-whisper, whether he really believed that Willy talks to the frog. Hugo, much to my surprise, said he didn't believe it for a moment; the whole thing, he said, was a practical joke — or else Willy was soft in the head; he didn't know which, and he didn't care. Batters said he was glad to hear it; he had been wondering whether he was the only sane man in the party.

C.J., who had overheard, spoke up for Willy. Darwin, he said, was more intelligent than a lot of people he knew, and certainly more sensible.

The result is that the crew is divided into two factions: an unhappy thing, and fraught with danger should an emergency arise. Disunity is the greatest danger that an expedition can encounter.

Between the Darwinians and the non-Darwinians, I myself take a middle course. I have reserved judgment. I remember a certain wildness in Willy's manner during the hurricane — especially his willingness to abandon the democratic principle in a moment of panic — and have to face the possibility that the search for the talking fish may be all a mistake. It is a disturbing thought, and has quite spoilt my enjoyment of the adventure.

Meanwhile, the daily routine continues. In our under-water trips we are no longer able to reach bottom, which Hugo interprets as a sign that we are in deep water. He is no longer able to supply Batters with seaweed, and grinds him up fish-bones instead. The resulting smell is even worse than its predecessor. Sea-water has got to the putty, which has gone hard and is almost unchewable. Hugo and Batters are delighted. After a fortnight of sawdust diet bark is beginning to grow on the backs of their hands.

The kittens are doing things at ten times the usual speed. They have a peculiar growth on their foreheads which Willy is unable to identify. It is made of bone and shaped like a spade. They get in everybody's way, and, although pretty, are a great nuisance. Willy suggested drowning some of them; and Batters, who is unable to defend himself from their playful attentions, strongly seconded the idea. C.J., who is fond of kittens, said he wouldn't hear of it, and Hugo, to my surprise, spoke up in support; it was, he said, bad luck to drown ships' cats; no seaman would dream of doing it. He said that if he caught anybody so much as laying a finger on a kitten he would ram his teeth down his windpipe.

This settled the practical issue; but it created a compli-cated situation, inasmuch as Hugo and Batters, who are allies over the Darwinian controversy, are enemies about the cats; and similarly for the other two. It also raised a difficult philosophical problem; for when I expressed sur-prise that Willy, an animal-lover, should be prepared to drown the kittens, he said that since this would save the lives of a lot of flying fish it was the humane thing to do. It seems to me that there is a fallacy in this argument, although I have been unable so far to locate it. In this matter as in the other dispute, I have reserved judgment; and the two together give me much food for thought.

Today, C.J. made radio contact with Equatorio, and we learned the exciting news that the first space-ship of the International Interplanetary Institute will be launched in a few weeks' time from an island in the Pacific. The space-ship, which is named *Argonaut,* is five hundred yards long and is being shipped from California in a specially-built carrier called the *Argus.* The project has cost a thousand million pounds. Willy says that with a bit of luck we might witness the take-off.

At lunch-time, Willy, going to change Neptune's milk, made an extraordinary discovery. One of the kittens had inserted its bony growth between the oyster's two shells and was twisting it sideways. Willy was beside himself with joy. Nature had invented an oyster-opener! It was, he said, an event of the first importance. It would revolutionise biological theory. It would get him his F.R.S. We congratulated him; but said that it was rather hard luck on Neptune. Willy agreed, and made a cage for him. He sits in his bowl of milk protected by the cage, which is surrounded by six prowling kittens. It is a pity that they have to be frustrated; but Neptune's safety comes first. Nature is a stern mother.

After lunch I decided to write another letter to my wife, and asked Hugo what the date was. He said that it depended on whether we had passed the international date line. He explained that people who travel round the world gain or lose a day, depending on which way round they go. I asked him if this meant that they became a day older or younger; but he said that this was not the case; it was difficult to explain why not, but it definitely was not so. I was relieved at this, but was still not very clear about it all.

Hugo explained that in order to avoid confusion, it had been agreed that a change of date should be made whenever a traveller crossed a certain line. This line went from North Pole to South Pole, passing through the Pacific. Irrespective of whether he had been round the world or not, the traveller added or subtracted a day to the date, depending on the direction in which he crossed the line.

It was, he said, a difficult thing to understand, and had caused endless trouble. Mariners had been worried by it for centuries. Illiterate captains had got into frightful trouble with the authorities for getting it wrong, and the date line was shunned by all seamen. There were a few old-fashioned skippers who still preferred to go right round the world rather than cross it. A party of explorers who had camped at the North Pole, and had consequently crossed the line every time they walked across the tent, had been driven mad trying to keep their postal records straight, and had ended by walking down the line into the sea.

But the Deep Sea Sufferers, said Hugo, took special courses in how to cross the line, and knew exactly what to do. When crossing from west to east one added a day; when crossing from east to west one subtracted it.

'No, no,' said Batters. 'The other way round, old boy.'

'Don't be silly, old boy,' said Hugo.

'Work it out for yourself, old boy. If you go round the world in a second, from west to east, you get a buckshee sunrise.'

'So you do if you go from east to west.'

'But in that case,' said C.J., 'the sun rises in the west.'

'What's that got to do with it?' said Willy. 'I agree with Hugo.'

'Don't be so stupid, mun,' said C.J.

I retired to the bows and tried to think it out for myself. I have a watch which registers the date; if I went round the world in a second the date wouldn't change, whatever direction I took. As far as I could see, the whole thing was a fallacy.

I mentioned this to the others, who told me I didn't know what I was talking about. They were all in a very bad temper. Willy and C.J. were drawing diagrams on the deck and quarrelling over them. Batters was muttering to himself in his hatch. Hugo was sulking in the stern. It was, I reflected, a black day in the history of navigation.

By supper-time heads had cooled; but an atmosphere of suspicion prevailed. It had been realised that there were now three unresolved issues aboard: the Darwinian disagreement, the kitten controversy and the date line dispute. Each of the four men had a different ally on each separate issue, but he quarrelled with him on the other two issues; the total effect being that everybody had twice as much reason to distrust everybody else as they had to trust them. The network of cross-alliances was too intricate to be visualised by any ordinary intelligence; and the result was chaos. Willy tried to draw a diagram; but they couldn't even agree about that; and another quarrel arose in which nobody had any allies at all. All of them seemed to consider me some kind of traitor, and I have seldom been so unhappy.

In the middle of it all the cats started doing things at fifteen times normal speed, and the ensuing conditions were indescribable.

This morning I was awakened by a loud booming noise. I rushed on deck, to find the rest of the crew already there. Over the western horizon flashes of light could be seen, each being followed by the sound of a heavy explosion.

'What is it?' I asked. 'A firework display?'

The cats, I noticed, were doing things at twenty times normal speed; and the things they were doing did not encourage optimism.

'It's the naval manoeuvres,' Willy explained. 'We seem to be drifting in their direction.'

'Isn't that rather a bad thing?' I said.

'Don't worry,' said Hugo. 'We've as much right here as they have.'

Just after daybreak we drifted into the combat zone. Ships of all kinds were steaming at top speed in all directions — corvettes, destroyers, cruisers, battleships and air-craft-carriers — all firing broadsides and blowing their sirens. Aeroplanes circled overhead, breaking the sound barrier. The noise was deafening.

I was getting somewhat worried about our safety, and was about to suggest running up a neutral flag, when all of a sudden the firing ceased.

'Perhaps they've run out of ammunition,' I said.

A motor-launch was making in our direction. It drew up alongside, and a smart naval Lieutenant hailed us. He seemed to be struggling with some strong emotion.

'Compliments of the Admiral,' he shouted; 'and what the blue blazes do you think you're doing?'

Willy explained that we were an expedition.

This seemed to annoy the Lieutenant. 'I didn't think you were a debating society,' he shouted. 'Where do you think you're going?'

Willy said that that was up to the Gumbolt current.

'You can't come this way,' said the Lieutenant. 'We're having a battle.'

'You can't stop us,' said Willy.

'Oh, can't I?' said the Lieutenant. 'We'll see about that.' He motioned his men to make fast to the *Talking Fish*. 'You're going to be towed out of the area.' He jumped aboard the raft.

'Oh no you don't,' said Hugo.

The Lieutenant had caught sight of Batters, who was visible at intervals beneath a group of affectionate kittens. 'What do you mean?' he said, staring.

'International law,' said Hugo. 'Article 38752, section XVIe, paragraph 28.'

The Lieutenant was still looking at Batters. 'What about it?' he said.

'This is international water,' Hugo explained. 'You can't touch us. You've already committed an act of piracy by coming aboard.'

The Lieutenant looked worried. 'Did you say . .?' he asked.

Hugo nodded.

'You don't mean it, old man?' said the Lieutenant, who seemed suddenly to have lost interest in Batters.

'I most certainly do,' said Hugo. 'I could have you hoisted from the yardarm for this.'

The Lieutenant was slightly green about the eyebrows. 'Look here, old chap,' he stammered; 'I didn't mean any harm.'

'Tell that to the court martial,' said Hugo.

'I have a wife and family,' said the Lieutenant.

'Should have thought about them before,' said Hugo.

'My old father,' said the Lieutenant: 'it would break him.'

'Let's get this clear,' said Hugo, in a shocked voice. 'You want us to overlook an act of piracy simply because you have an old father. Is that it?'

'Well . . .' said the Lieutenant.

'What do you take us for?' said Hugo.

The Lieutenant gestured helplessly.

'Anyway,' said Hugo; 'what are *you* doing here — making all this bloody noise and interfering with innocent expeditions?'

'We're defending freedom,' the Lieutenant whispered.

'What's that?' shouted Hugo. 'Speak up, man!'

'Defending freedom,' repeated the Lieutenant. 'Sir.'

'That's better!' said Hugo. 'So you're defending freedom, are you?'

'Yes, sir,' said the Lieutenant.

'And we,' said Hugo, 'are practising it.'

'Bravo!' I murmured.

Hugo stroked his beard. 'As far as I can see,' he said to the trembling Lieutenant, 'you haven't a leg to stand on. I doubt whether any lawyer would risk his reputation by defending you.'

The Lieutenant looked at him with large, appealing eyes.

'But don't take my word for it,' said Hugo. 'Ask any of these gentlemen.'

We nodded solemnly.

'Please, sir,' said the Lieutenant, 'couldn't you possibly overlook it this once?'

Hugo frowned.

'It won't occur again, sir,' said the Lieutenant. His mouth was quivering.

Hugo looked at us. 'What do you think, chaps?'

We rubbed our jaws. 'He seems a decent fellow,' said Willy, hesitatingly.

'Has a generous nose,' I said.

'Headstrong, though,' said C.J.

'Inquisitive puppy!' cried Batters, in a muffled voice.

Hugo turned to the Lieutenant. 'Look here,' he said: 'It would be an inconvenience to us to give evidence. We'll say no more about it.'

'Oh thank you, sir!' said the Lieutenant. He hesitated. 'Well, sir, I think I had better be getting along.'

'Yes,'. said Hugo. 'Why don't you?'

'By the way,' he said, as they were casting off. 'I wonder if you can settle an argument. When you cross the international date line from east to west, do you add a day, or subtract it?'

'It's quite easy, sir,' said the Lieutenant. 'You. . .' He frowned. 'I'll ask the Admiral, sir; he's sure to know.'

As he moved off he glanced again at Batters, and shook his head.

When the Lieutenant had gone we crowded round Hugo and congratulated him on his masterly handling of a difficult situation. We were a happy and united party again; and the contrast with our recent state of disunity was so great that Willy flung his arms round C.J.'s neck in a moment of affection, and Hugo struck me heavily on the shoulder, pitching me head-first into Batters' hatchway. Batters' head, I found, was as solid as it looked. Hugo roared with laughter and said it was time Batters and I put our heads together, anyway.

Just before lunch-time the Lieutenant returned. 'The Admiral's compliments,' he said. 'He is consulting the Admiralty about your case; in the meantime, you are permitted to drift.'

'My compliments to the Admiral,' said Hugo. 'He has my permission to carry on with his consultation. What about the date line?'

'He's looking into it,' said the Lieutenant.

We spent the day quietly, drifting across the combat zone. The fleet had dropped anchor and was doing its washing. We exchanged friendly banter with the sailors as we passed, and Darwin became so excited that he fell head-first into a tin of treacle.

At lunch-time Hugo intercepted a Morse signal from the Admiral's ship. He said that the Admiral was asking the Commander-in-Chief about the date line.

An aircraft-carrier signalled in reply. ' "Commander-in-Chief's compliments to the Admiral",' read Hugo.

' "When travelling from east to west a day is subtracted." '

'There you are!' he said. 'What did I tell you?'

'There's another signal,' said C.J., pointing to the horizon. 'What does it say?'

'Nothing important,' said Hugo.

' "Rear-Admiral's compliments to the Commander-in-Chief",' cried Batters from his hatch. ' "Is he to understand that the Commander-in-Chief is in the habit of sailing backwards?" '

'Damned fool!' said Hugo. 'What's that got to do with it?'

The aircraft-carrier was replying: 'Commander-in-Chief's compliments to the Rear-Admiral. Commander-in-Chief is referring the matter to the Admiralty. Rear-Admiral had better watch his stripes.'

At six bells we learnt from the radio that the question of our free passage through the battle area had aroused a ferment in diplomatic circles. Foreign Secretaries had been recalled from holiday and Cabinets had held emergency meetings. Meanwhile, we continued to drift slowly past the stationary ships; and the fleet continued with its washing.

For the first time for several days there were no arguments aboard the raft. By tacit agreement we avoided controversial matters and discussed only those things that we could agree about. We had a very quiet evening.

In the morning we found ourselves alone in the ocean. We had drifted out of the combat zone. Loud explosions in the east told us that the fleet was once more defending freedom.

I am not happy about the future. At breakfast-time Aristotle gave birth to a second litter of spade-headed kittens, and the raft is no longer the peaceful place it used to be. It was a great relief to escape below for our morning's work, during which we made friends with a stable of seahorses and did the routine inspection of Batters' hull. His kneecaps are badly wrinkled, but they are the only part of him below the water-line that is not encrusted by sea creatures. Two more sucker-fish had attached themselves during the night and a third was swimming about looking for an opening. We have given up trying to count the barnacles. He is far too crusted by modern standards; his bottom should have been scraped weeks ago; but he won't hear of having it done until we dock. His toes are in poor condition, having been much nibbled by sharks; he has a tough time fighting them off, but says it keeps him fit. Willy has taken some photographs of him with his underwater camera; he says they will cause a sensation in Belgrave Square, and I dare say he is right. Above water, Batters is less interesting, although twigs have started to grow out of his ears. He keeps wonderfully cheerful, but is inclined to patronise Hugo, who can find very little to suffer about and is consequently restless. He particularly envies Batters his twigs, and examines his own ears a dozen times a day. He has worked out our position, which is Toronto or Winnipeg; he is not sure which. I am writing my journal, and Willy is blowing Neptune's nose and changing the milk. I ask him how the pearl is coming along. 'Nicely,' he says; and I nod approvingly. C.J. is asleep; how he does it, with kittens scrambling all over him, I just don't know.

We have been discussing the *Argus,* which, Hugo says, should now be in these latitudes. We hope very much to see her, if not actually to witness the take-off of the *Argonaut.* Willy says that, with a bit of luck, she might be willing to take the cats off our hands.

Two days ago, the shoal of fish which accompanies the raft everywhere was joined by a huge white whale, which Hugo says has a familiar look. It has examined us from all angles, and seems particularly interested in Hugo. Although rather alarming in appearance, it has done us no harm, except to drench us from time to time with a cloud of oily vapour.

We now speak Buburup like natives, and 'blum-blum' has become the accepted greeting for all occasions. Willy thinks that Neptune may be picking it up; he splashes his milk to Willy at breakfast-time, and Willy believes he is trying to say 'good-morning'. His pronunciation is very bad, however, and C.J., who firmly believes it all, has suggested a stiffer mixture of condensed milk, which he thinks would have better acoustic properties. Hugo and Batters shake their heads and look meaningly at each other; and I find myself still unable to make up my mind. I am convinced of Willy's sincerity, but have doubts about his judgment.

We often discuss our prospects of finding the talking fish. Hugo and Batters are of course openly derisive; and even Willy is beginning to lose hope. He thinks we may have drifted off course, and has asked me if I would consider trying again next year. I told him I doubted whether my commitments would allow it.

Later. My forebodings have been justified. Towards evening five of the original litter of kittens, who are now fully grown cats, gave birth to six apiece. Willy sat down with a slide-rule and a worried look and worked out the consequences. The cats, he says, are operating according to the exponential law: something like compound interest, only more so. He estimates that in a week's time there will be four thousand of them. He doesn't see how the resources of the expedition can stand it.

We had a violent discussion about what to do. As before, Willy and Batters are for throwing the cats overboard, and Hugo and C.J. against it. I am in two minds, and frantic with worry; if what Willy says is right, some of the cats will certainly starve to death, which is not a nice thought. Challenged by the others to make up my mind, I said that as far as I could see the only thing to do was to abandon raft and let nature solve the problem in her own way. Everybody said that this was cowardly evasion, which I thought rather unfair.

We have failed to reach agreement; and I can only pray that heaven will reveal a solution. Meanwhile, the rate of activity has become unbelievable, and I am feeling a little dizzy. Darwin's cage has been slung from the rigging, out of reach of the cats, and Neptune has been put in with his friend. The cats are expressing their frustration at the top of their voices.

What a strange day! I shall never forget it. Every detail is as clear in my memory as if it were carved in stone.

After a night made miserable by cats and nightmares I drifted, in the first warmth of the morning sun, into a refreshing sleep, from which I awoke gently to a heavenly silence broken only by the cheerful lapping of water and the word 'blum-blum . . . blum-blum' repeated over and over again in a voice I had not heard before.

I thought at first that Neptune had mastered his pronunciation at last; but I soon realised that the sound was coming from beneath me.

The talking fish!

I jumped to my feet. The cats were asleep in the bows. The crew were snoring in the stern. I roused them; and in a few seconds we were all running around in circles, getting in each other's way as we rushed for the underwater gear. The cats joined in, tangling themselves in the apparatus, spitting and scratching at us when we tried to release them. Tripping over a kitten, C.J. ran his head against a bulwark and had to be talked to kindly for a few minutes. Willy was dancing with impatience and getting his straps twisted. Hugo helped him to fasten them, and nearly strangled him.

At last we slid over the side and submerged. The fish crowded round as usual, and a few old friends came for their customary titbit. We swam among them, looking for a new species and calling: 'blum-blum'. The fish moved slowly to let us pass; most of them were quite used to us and treated us like one of themselves. The whale watched us from a distance.

Suddenly, there was a flurry. The fish turned in one direction and darted away, leaving us alone and alarmed in the ocean. Even the whale had disappeared.

Instinctively, we came close together and looked around. What could it be?

'Look!' cried Willy pointing; and we saw that some large eels were approaching. 'Look!' cried C.J.; and we saw that more eels were approaching from the other direction. 'Look!' cried Hugo; and we saw that eels were approaching from above. 'Look!' I cried, and pointed out dozens of eels below us.

They were about six feet long and eight inches in diameter. They were dark blue in colour, with white stripes of varying numbers around their middles. They had sharp teeth and impassive expressions.

They formed a sphere around us; we were completely surrounded by eels.

'It's all right,' said Willy. 'Eels are friendly creatures.' His teeth were chattering.

'Wait till you see the whites of their eyes,' said Hugo.

'What do we do then?' muttered C.J.

Inside the sphere was a single eel, larger than the rest, with longer teeth and more stripes. He swam towards us, then suddenly turned and moved off again. He did this three times, then turned and motioned with his head.

'I think he wants us to follow him,' said Willy.

'Don't move,' said Hugo. 'We'll call their bluff.'

The large eel was now moving away slowly, and we noticed that the sphere of eels was following his movement. We were no longer in the centre.

'Keep quite still,' said Hugo.

The nearest eels were about three feet away when we were suddenly convulsed by an electric shock, which left us shaken and panic-stricken. 'Electric eels!' cried Willy. 'I'm off!' He darted for the centre of the sphere, and we followed. No more shocks came; and we swam behind the large eel, keeping a distance of six feet or so. The other eels moved with us, keeping us always at their centre.

We discussed in whispers what we should do. 'Better not antagonise them,' said Hugo. 'We must find a method of using our superior intelligence.'

Our course was downwards at a gentle angle. We had travelled for some minutes when we came to the sea bottom, which at this point was a level stretch of sand broken by seaweed-covered outcrops of rock. We moved towards the base of one of these small cliffs, and the sphere of eels parted, forming an irregularly-shaped cage bounded on two sides by cliff and sand and on the others by eels. The large eel took up a vertical position facing the rock.

Into this enclosure swam a large fish; it must have been over five feet long and about ten stone in weight. It came to rest with its tail towards the cliff and looked at us with cold fishy eyes.

'Blum-blum,' it said.

'Good God!' said Hugo.

'Blum-blum,' said Willy, beaming all over his face.

'I understand,' said the fish, speaking in Buburup, 'that you speak our language.'

'Yes,' said Willy. 'I got it from the inhabitants of . . .'

'You will please confine yourself to answering questions,' said the fish. 'What is your number, rank and name?'

'My what?' said Willy.

'Number, rank and name,' repeated the fish.

C

'My name is Willy Wagstaff,' said Willy. 'I haven't any number and rank.'

'Lies, of course,' said the fish. He looked deliberately at each of us in turn; and I shuddered as I read the message in his unpitying eye.

'Let us understand each other,' he said at last. 'You are spies sent here by the human race, which is planning to invade our territory.'

'No!' cried Willy. 'It's not true!'

'You are not the first,' the fish continued. 'Seaings by men like yourselves have been reported from many parts of the ocean. So far, operations have been confined to physical assault or attempted bribery. You are the first to come among us as spies, speaking our language and hoping to learn our secrets.'

'No!' said Willy again. 'Why should we want to invade you?'

'It is well known,' said the fish, 'that humans kill for enjoyment. Is it not true that you breed fishes for the purpose of putting them into rivers to be caught?'

'Only the civilised nations,' said Willy.

'Yes,' said the fish. 'We have heard about civilisation. Is it not the civilised humans who poison the sea with oil and make these terrible explosions?'

'Well . . .' said Willy.

'Civilisation must be an awful thing,' said the fish. 'Can nothing be done to prevent it?'

'Some of us think rather highly of it,' I said.

'I can only conclude,' said the fish, 'that your minds must be immature. But we are wasting time. Do you deny having come here as forerunners of a human invasion?'

'Of course,' I said.

'In that case, what are you doing here?'

Willy explained the purpose of the expedition.

'I see,' said the fish. 'When you publish your story, other humans will no doubt visit us?'

'Certainly.'

'They will kill some of our people?'

'No,' said Willy. 'At least, I hope not.'

'You hope not!' said the fish. 'Will they take some of us prisoner?'

'Well — ' said Willy.

'Precisely!' said the fish, sternly. 'You are clearly guilty as charged.'

'No!' we all cried.

'Yes!' said the fish. 'If you think it over in your immature minds you will realise I am right. Can you give any good reason why you should not be executed?'

'I have an old father,' said Hugo. 'It would break him.'

'You should have thought of that before,' said the fish.

'I have a book to write,' I said.

'You can do it through a medium.'

'I'm not fit to die,' said C.J.

'That is your problem. You are certainly not fit to live.'

'I have a dependent oyster,' said Willy.

'A likely story!' said the fish. 'Your excuses are typical of your immature minds. You are condemned to be electrocuted. Sentence will be carried out as soon as the guards have charged their condensers. We like to make it a quick death; it is pleasanter for all concerned.'

We looked at each other helplessly.

'In the meantime,' said the fish, 'please make yourselves at home.'

The sea was filled with a deep throbbing note, like the hum of a power-station. The eels were making great efforts; their bodies were stiff with strain.

'Nice weather we're having,' said the fish.

'Oh yes,' said Willy.

'I hope you had a nice trip?'

'Pretty fair,' said Willy.

'Nothing like travel for broadening the mind,' said the fish. 'That's what I always say.'

'Quite,' said Willy.

'Did a lot of travelling myself, in my young days.'

'Really?'

'Visited the North Sea, once.'

'How nice,' said Willy.

'That was in '32,' said the fish. '1832, I mean. The Panama canal wasn't built then. Had to go round Cape Horn.

'Those were the days!' he added.

'I'm sure they were,' said Willy.

'I'm not boring you, am I?'

'Not at all,' said Willy. 'Do go on.'

'Had a chap with us,' said the fish: 'name of Bubble.' He chuckled. 'Silly name, that! Never met such a chap. You'd have liked him '

'I'm sure I would,' said Willy.

'Where was I?' said the fish.

'Chap name of Bubble,' said Willy.

'Oh yes. You never met him did you?'

'I don't think I did.'

'Pity,' said the fish. 'You'd have liked him. Never met such a chap.' He chuckled.

'That was in '32,' he added.

'Mind you,' he said, 'things were different in those days.' He sighed. 'I've enjoyed our little talk. If there's anything I can do for you, just mention it.'

'It's good of you,' said Willy. 'There was one thing.'

'Just mention it, old chap.'

'Well,' said Willy: 'we're being followed by a large white whale who keeps throwing oil over us. I wonder if you could get him to stop it? It spoils our washing.'

'That must be Moby Charlie,' said the fish. 'He comes of an unfortunate family. He's a bit simple, but perfectly harmless. Be nice to him; it might restore his faith in human nature.'

'We'll do that,' said Willy. 'But what about the oil?'

'I'll have a word with him. It's probably only nervousness.'

'Very decent of you,' said Willy.

'Not at all,' said the fish. 'Only too glad to do it. Well: I see the guards are charged up. I'd better be getting along. Look after yourself.'

In a flash he had turned away and whisked out of the cage. The eels had reformed their sphere and were coming closer. Their smooth bodies gleamed with static electricity, soon to be released as deadly current. Sparks flashed from their spiky teeth. Voltmeters in their foreheads quivered about the danger mark.

We held a hurried consultation. Hugo was inclined to take a high line. He said that one Englishman was as good as a hundred ruddy fish. Willy said that even an Englishman was no good against a thousand volts. He glanced at a voltmeter. 'Five thousand,' he amended. C.J. said that perhaps there was some way of short-circuiting the eels and blowing their fuses.

Nearer and nearer came the eels. They were now lit up from within by the intensity of their charge. Lightning flashed between them when they came too close together. The needles of their voltmeters were wrapped around the infinity stop.

c*

'This is it, chaps,' said Hugo. 'Let's show them how Englishmen can die.'

C.J. looked at him indignantly. 'There you go again,' he said, 'insulting the Welsh.'

'Sorry, old chap,' said Hugo. 'Let's show them how Britons can die.'

'That's better,' said C.J.

The eels were scarcely a yard away. Their skins were sizzling. I tried to ignore them and think of my dear wife, so soon to be a widow. I thought of the happy times we had had together and the winter woollies she would be knitting for my return.

There was a blinding flash, and a shock of pain convulsed me. Every muscle went rigid, and my cry of distress was strangled in a voiceless throat.

'Sorry, old boy,' said Hugo.

I opened my eyes. I was lying on the deck of the raft. Hugo had dropped a barometer on my head and was examining it for damage.

It had all been a dream.

I am writing this on top of my cabin, where we have re-
treated to escape the cats. They are now feet deep on the
deck, doing things more quickly than ever. Somewhere
amidst the seething mass kittens are being born at an un-
precedented rate, and Batters is getting all the suffering
he could ask for. There is nothing we can do about it.
Even if we could agree to throw them overboard it is too
late to do so; they have turned vicious, and it is as much
as we can do to defend ourselves against them. At their
present rate of breeding they will overflow us in a day or
two, and that will be the end.

We discuss the possibilities of escape. Willy hopes the
cats will start falling into the sea; but so far they show no
sign of doing so. Hugo puts his faith in our finding an
island. He has found one on his chart and says that for all
he knows it might be just over the horizon. C.J. says we
ought to prepare our souls for the worst; he is preparing
his in the middle of the roof, out of reach of the jumping
cats. I try to do the same; but with little success. I have
just discovered an unsuspected weakness in my character.
I find that although I would not want to have drowned
the cats myself I should be a great deal happier than I am
if Willy had drowned them. I cannot reconcile this with
my philosophy; and until I have done so I shall not be fit
to die.

The truth has been kept from Neptune; but he senses
our mood and is an unhappy oyster. His depression has
communicated itself to Darwin, and they sit in their cage

like two small monuments of misery. The pearl is quite off-colour, and the milk has curdled.

Moby Charlie has deserted us, which seems like an omen. I fear that the end is very close. Only a miracle can save us.

The miracle has occurred! This morning, sweeping the horizon with his sextant, Hugo sighted an island. Making a quick calculation, he announced land ho. 'Where away?' said Willy. 'Three points on the starboard quarter,' said Hugo, consulting his charts. 'All hands on roof!' cried Willy; and we sprang to our feet.

And land it was: a long dark line between sea and sky, which became a coast of precipitous cliffs as we approached.

We congratulated Hugo on a fine piece of navigation and prepared for the landing. It was agreed that we should put the cats ashore and make a quick escape. I was not happy about the consequences to the inhabitants of the island; but the others had no scruples; they said that our first responsibility was towards our loved ones, and the island was almost certainly uninhabited anyway. I was not altogether convinced by this argument, but was over-ruled by democratic vote.

The cliffs loomed higher, and our hopes rose with them. But as we came near we saw that the course of the current had changed, and that we would drift past the north-east corner of the island.

After the excitement of the preceding hour this was a cruel blow. We stood in despair, watching the rocks move past barely a cable's length away. With the cats almost at roof level we could do nothing to save ourselves.

Then there was a call from Batters: 'Bottom ho!'

'*What* ho?' shouted Willy.

'Bottom,' said Batters. 'I've touched bottom.'

'You're not the only one,' said Willy.

'No, no,' said Batters. 'The bottom of the sea.'

We looked at each other with new hope.

'Run for the shore!' cried Hugo; and we felt the raft move against the current. Some distance away waves were breaking on a sloping shelf of rock. We cheered Batters on, and the shelf drew nearer and nearer. At the last moment a large wave threatened to sweep us away; but Batters gave a cry of triumph and the raft scraped against the rock. 'All cats ashore!' cried Willy; and the tumbling mass of cats poured on to the rock and raced for the land. As the last cat left us Batters was dragged from his hold, and we swept out again to sea.

For three days we have drifted in quiet water, moving slowly past the north coast of the island, enjoying the old routine. Now that I can think of other things besides cats, my mind keeps returning to my dream. It is as vivid in my memory as an actual experience, and I have to keep reminding myself that it did not really happen. The result is that I have begun to doubt other experiences. My journal confirms that earlier events on the *Talking Fish* did really happen; but I have no means of checking on other episodes in my career. My companions are of little help. I asked them whether I had once climbed a very high mountain, but they were unable to agree about it. Willy says he is almost certain he remembers something of the kind; he thinks he read about it in the *Buburup Weekly Advertiser*. C.J. says he is probably thinking of the Everest expedition; and Hugo says that if it had been true he would certainly have heard about it. It is all very confusing. I see from my journal, however, that I really am married; and this is a great comfort. I am sure my dear wife will help me to put my memory in order.

I am worried about the ethics of the expedition. It seems to me that we really are the advance-guard of a human invasion; and this is a terrible thing. Willy says I worry too much; it is all in the cause of science. Hugo says I have nothing to worry about; there is no earthly chance of our finding the talking fish. I hope he is right.

I worry also about the cats. If the island is inhabited the consequences may be disastrous for the inhabitants. In any case, it is likely to be disastrous for the cats; what will happen when the island is overrun with them? It is a matter for the United Nations; but we have no means of letting them know about it. According to Willy's calculations there should already be fifty thousand cats, and it is clearly an emergency.

The others are strangely unconcerned, which I hope does not indicate a callous nature on anybody's part, but only a lack of imagination. They are enjoying the cruise. Hugo has a leaf sprouting from his forehead and is as happy as our comfortable circumstances will allow. Batters has fought a great battle with three sharks, and is inclined to boast. C.J. is now like a round brown berry. He and Darwin have started singing hymns together, and are practising for the Eisteddfod. Neptune is looking the picture of health; his pearl has picked up again and is once more coming along nicely. The two animals have grown very fond of each other during their captivity, which speaks volumes for their strength of character. Willy has had a long talk with Darwin, who said that he was beginning to understand Neptune's language and might be able to act as interpreter. Willy was naturally delighted; but Hugo and Batters shook their heads sadly.

18   *An Appalling Thing has Happened*

An appalling thing has happened: so terrible that words are quite inadequate. My hand trembles as I write; and my mind flinches as it recapitulates the events of this disastrous day.

Yesterday we learnt from the radio that the *Argus* was nearing its destination. The eyes of the whole world were upon it. Man was about to make his first pioneering adventure into the tremendous unknown which surrounds this little earth of ours. The project was an international one; there was not a single nation which had not contributed. In more ways than one the *Argus* was the symbol of a new age.

This afternoon we were drifting quietly parallel to the cliffs when C.J. drew our attention to a ship which had appeared over the horizon. As it drew nearer we saw that it was no ordinary vessel. It was nearly half a mile long and proportionately high. It had none of the usual superstructures, but above the rail could be seen the top edge of what appeared to be an enormous metal cylinder.

The *Argus*! It could be nothing else.

She maintained an oblique course until about a mile away, then turned and made straight towards us; and it occurred to me at once that this island must be the one from which the space-ship was to be launched. I looked round, and saw that we were drifting towards a wide opening which had appeared in the cliffs. In a few minutes we had entered a magnificent natural harbour. It must have been two miles across, and was surrounded by high cliffs which fell vertically into the sea, suggesting a considerable depth of water. The absence of surf confirmed this impression. Only in the very centre of the harbour was there any indication of shallow water; here a single jagged rock rose from the sea like the spear of some malevolent submarine deity.

At one side of the harbour, where the cliffs were at their lowest, a large quay had been built. On it were two colossal cranes, and behind was a group of buildings. A line of men stood on the edge of the quay, looking towards the harbour entrance.

And in the entrance appeared the nose of the *Argus,* towering above us and threatening to run us down.

'Lifeboat stations!' cried Willy, leaping in all directions. I ran to get my journal; but in my excitement I tripped over a bollard and fell head-first into the sea.

I came to the surface to see Hugo doubled up with laughter. 'It's all *right!*' he spluttered. 'Power must give way to sail.'

Figures had appeared at the bow of the *Argus,* and we heard the cry 'Sail ho!' 'Where away?' came a distant voice. 'Dead ahead!' was the reply. 'Give way to sail!' came the order; and the *Argus* swung round, missing us by feet.

Her wake hit me like a tidal wave, hurling me against the raft. I sustained a severe blow on the temple, but held on, and was hauled aboard by Hugo, who was still chuckling.

During this episode some subconscious anxiety had been troubling me. Now that the emergency was over I realised what it was.

'The cats!' I cried.

'Where?' said Willy, looking round.

'No, no,' I said. 'We must warn the *Argus*.'

Willy turned pale. 'They mustn't dock,' he muttered. 'If those cats get aboard . . .'

The *Argus* was moving smoothly past. Lines of washing were hung up to dry, and sailors with soap-suds to their elbows were leaning over the rail looking down on us.

I waved them with both hands to keep away from the island. I put my hands together as if in prayer, then pointed out to sea.

The crew waved back cheerfully. Soap-suds drifted down on us like a midsummer snowstorm.

'You mustn't dock!' cried Willy. 'There are millions of cats on the island!'

The crew roared with laughter.

'They're operating according to the exponential law,' shouted Willy.

The crew held its sides.

'I have proof,' said Willy, waving a piece of graph paper.

'Stick it up your jumper!' cried a wit.

I realised suddenly that the ship's change of course was taking her directly towards the vicious rock in the centre of the harbour. It seemed that catastrophe was imminent. But at the last moment she swung round in the reverse turn and headed for the quay. Still thinking of the cats, I seized a saucepan and tried to paddle after the ship; but I succeeded only in turning the raft in a circle. The others started walking round the deck in order to keep opposite the *Argus*. I called them to help with the paddling; but C.J., who was leading, and was not looking where he was going, walked overboard. The others followed, and I was left alone on the raft.

In such emergencies the true adventurer discovers hidden reserves of initiative. It flashed across my mind that I had once been a boy scout and had learned the semaphore code. Jumping to my feet, I began to signal with my arms, spelling out the word 'Danger!' A group of sailors were watching from the stern, and I was confident that they would understand the message. But they must have been unqualified seamen, for they took no notice of my signals. The *Argus* continued on her course, and in a few minutes she was alongside the quay and ropes were being made fast by the shore party.

The others climbed aboard, and we drifted towards the *Argus*. So far there had been no sign of the cats. But suddenly Willy gave a cry, and pointed frantically.

Behind the landing-area was a low grassy hill. Over its brow a stream of cats was pouring: many cats; more cats than I had seen in the whole of my life; angry cats; wild and deplorable cats, racing towards the *Argus,* spitting and howling as they came.

It was a terrible sight. I clutched Willy's arm and gasped with horror. Surely nothing could save the crew of the *Argus* from a gruesome fate.

But the cats had been seen. From the ship came a loud cry: 'Cats ho!'

'Where away?' was the reply.

'Dead ahead!'

'Cast off!' came the order; and in the nick of time the ropes were thrown off, the ship's engines raced, and the *Argus* backed quickly from the quay.

Simultaneously, the shore party flung itself as one man into the sea.

Again the raft was in danger. The *Argus* was racing backwards towards us. Her stern loomed up like an advancing cliff. Her screws churned the sea like a giant's washing-machine.

'It's all right,' said Hugo. 'Power must give way to sail.'

And sure enough, from above came the order: 'Give way to sail!' The *Argus* swung round, missing us by inches. The raft tossed in her wake like a mad thing, throwing us head-over-heels into the offing.

Staggering to our feet, we saw that the ship was steaming full speed for the rock. Her stern towered over the sharp and deadly pinnacle.

'Jack Robinson!' cried Willy; but he was too late. With a fearful crash the *Argus* impaled herself on the rock, thrusting her stern high as her impetus carried her forward, tearing her steel sides like paper. For a moment she hung transfixed, then slid seaward again, doing more damage as she returned to her element.

She settled with a heavy list. Water was pouring into her, and we felt the raft being carried towards her by the current. Soon we would be swept through the hole in her side, and would sink with her.

'Starboard all braces!' cried Willy; and C.J. began to fiddle with his trousers. Darwin croaked loudly. 'What's that?' said Willy. Darwin repeated his remark. 'Don't be silly, old chap,' said Willy. 'There aren't any pumps on a raft.'

He stuffed both animals into his pocket, together with a few tins of condensed milk. Hugo drew his knife and went to release Batters. The tough creepers resisted, and the knife blade broke. Hugo tore frantically with his fingers, while C.J. and I made parcels of our private belongings. I glanced upward. Boats were being launched from the ship and washing was hurriedly being taken in

Sea was pouring into the ship at a great rate. Hugo was still pulling at the creepers. C.J. had seized the lifebelt and was struggling to get inside it. I had lost my pyjama bottoms. Willy was searching the index of *The Sailor's Vade-Mecum*.

Batters came free at last. He climbed aboard and shook hands all round. 'Wouldn't have missed this for an hour in a torture-chamber,' he said.

The hole in the *Argus* was gaping around us like a hungry mouth. The *Talking Fish* gave a lurch and plunged into the bowels of the ship. 'Splice the sextant!' cried Willy; and we threw ourselves into the sea.

Somehow we managed to swim away. At a safe distance we turned to watch events. The *Argus* was low in the water. The boats were pulling away. We were hauled aboard one of them, which contained the Commander of the *Argus*. He said he was busy at present, but would like to speak to us later.

In a few minutes it was all over. The *Argus* raised her stern in the air and plunged into the depths of the sea. All round the harbour howls of rage and frustration came from thousands of feline throats.

The Commander turned to us with a kindly smile. 'Let's have a friendly little chat,' he said, 'shall we?'

He was a large man, with a deep and powerful voice which he made the most of. He was patting the gunwale of the boat, as if to assure it that there was not a thing in the world to get excited about: that he loved it as if it were his very own gunwale and would protect it from the harsh world.

He closed his eyes for a moment and took a deep breath before opening the conversation.

He said that it had been a rare privilege meeting us. He said he could see at a glance that we were gentle souls who would not hurt a fly. He said there was a kind of innocence in our faces which must be an inspiration to all who knew us. He said we must have thousands of friends. He said we had a spiritual quality which restored his faith in human nature.

I said he overestimated us.

'No, no!' he said, raising a protesting hand. He said he knew true quality when he saw it. He saw that we were as modest as we were good.

But, he said, we weren't to think that he idolised us. Far from it. He was a practical man. He did not expect perfection. There was, he admitted, one small matter in which he found us not beyond reproach.

I begged him to tell us what it was.

He said he would do so, much as it pained him to mention it. He said it might give us our chance to perfect ourselves. In years to come we would thank him for having been open with us.

He said he would not mention the years of labour which had gone into the building of the *Argonaut*: the sleepless nights of selfless boffins, the devoted labour of countless craftsmen, the untiring efforts of strike-negotiators. He would say nothing about the thousand million pounds -- the pocket-scrapings of dedicated shareholders -- which had made this tremendous project possible. He would pass over the hopes of millions of ordinary people the whole world over: people of every colour, creed and nation, who were united, for the first time in history, in a high and common adventure.

These were small things, he said; things of the world; important perhaps to the petty-minded, but not to be mentioned to noble creatures like ourselves. He would not mention them.

But there was, he said, one thing which he could not avoid mentioning, although it broke his heart to do so.

The Commander took another deep breath. He seemed to be fighting some inner urge. He had gone quite purple in the face and was steaming at the mouth. He was punching the gunwale as if he hated it for some shameful betrayal.

Then he exploded. He gave a wild cry, jumped to his feet and stabbed his forefinger repeatedly in our direction. 'What the rumbling thunderbolts,' he roared, 'do you mean by sinking my ship on washing day?'

Then he collapsed. He sank on to a thwart, put his hands over his face and sobbed.

It was understandable. He had been through a lot that day. I patted him on the shoulder and said he mustn't be ashamed of showing his feelings; they were part of his large-hearted nature. I said it was generous of him to say nothing about those other things, but we really didn't deserve it. I said that if he was short of underwear I could lend him some of mine; it seemed to be the kind that stretches.

He gave a kind of sobbing moan, and I saw that he appreciated my offer. 'Leave me alone!' he cried, rocking backwards and forwards.

'All right, old chap,' I said. 'If there's anything we can do, just say the word.'

He groaned pitifully.

'By the way,' Hugo said to him: 'there's something you might be able to help us on.'

The Commander raised a tear-stained face. 'Anything!' he said earnestly. 'Anything at all.'

'When you cross the international date line,' said Hugo, 'do you add a day or subtract one?'

'Let me see,' said the Commander, sniffing. 'You add one, don't you?' He gave Hugo a kindly smile and nodded. 'Yes; I'm sure that's right; you add one.'

'But,' said Hugo, 'it depends which way you go.'

'Oh yes,' said the Commander. 'It does, doesn't it?' He was searching for his handkerchief. I offered him mine.

'No, no,' he said. 'I couldn't.'

'Please do,' I said, and pressed it on him. He blew his nose loudly and offered me the handkerchief back. Then he thought better of it, and put it away, blushing. 'Forgive me,' he said. 'I'm not the man I was.'

'Never mind,' I said kindly. 'Just sit back and rest.'

'No,' he said. 'I have something on my mind. What was it?'

'The *Argonaut*?' I suggested.

'No. Something important.'

'Your family?'

'I haven't one. At least, I don't think I have.'

'Animal, vegetable or mineral?' I said.

'Vegetable!' cried the Commander. 'Something about fruit — figs, I think.'

'Not dates?' I suggested.

'That's it! Something about dates!'

'The international date line,' I said. 'Hugo asked you about it.'

'I remember,' said the Commander. 'It all comes back to me now. It depends which way you go, doesn't it?'

'That's right,' I said. 'You're doing very well.'

'We must get this settled,' said the Commander. He frowned, and nodded his head. 'Mr Twinkle will know!' He stood up and hailed one of the other boats, which drew up alongside.

'Mr Twinkle,' said the Commander: 'Our friends here have a little problem. I thought you might be able to help us. When you cross the equator, do you add a day, or subtract it?'

'Not the equator,' said Hugo. 'The international date line.'

'That's it!' said the Commander. 'I was nearly right, wasn't I?'

'Very nearly,' I said, patting his shoulder. He looked at me gratefully.

Mr Twinkle said he wasn't quite sure, but Mr Grudge would know. 'Fetch him, then,' said the Commander, 'there's a good chap.' He pressed my hand. 'We'll get to the bottom of this,' he said; 'I promise you.'

'It's very good of you,' I said.

'No, no,' he said hurriedly. 'It's a little thing, after all you've done.'

Mr Grudge said he had his own theory about the date line, but it wasn't ready for publication. He said that Mr

Brightly would be sure to know; he had been working on the subject for years.

Mr Brightly said that he had once been quite certain of the answer; but as his outlook matured he had had Doubts. He advised us to ask Mr Bowswinger.

It was late evening when Mr Twinkle suggested that we ought to be on our way to America. The Commander said he had no objection in principle, but he didn't see how we were to do it without abandoning the enquiry. All the boats were now huddled together, and the conference was proceeding at the top of everybody's voice. Those near the perimeter had to have things repeated for them, which made for difficulty.

Mr Twinkle proposed that the chief officers should transfer to the Commander's boat, so that the enquiry could continue during the voyage. The Commander was delighted with the suggestion; he said he would recommend Mr Twinkle for promotion.

The transfer was made, and we set off at last on our long journey. As we looked back at the island the dark cliffs were fringed with a moving silhouette of cats.

We settled down quickly to our new life. Batters had been unable to sit comfortably, and had asked to be put into the sea. A rope was tied around his neck and he was lowered over the stern. He said it was like getting home again. The tree-like condition of himself and Hugo was a source of interest to everybody. With the resumption of a normal diet their leaves had begun to wither; but the Commander kindly gave them a broken oar to eat, and they soon picked up again. Both had grown blossoms, and there was much speculation about whether they would fertilise each other.

Neptune had been installed in a tin of milk and was

making quite a name for himself. According to Willy, the two animals were now able to talk to each other; so that Darwin could act as interpreter between Willy and Neptune. Finding that his pearl was greatly admired by his shipmates, Neptune announced that he would be open to sightseers from ten to six, and two to six on Sundays. A small fee would be charged, the proceeds to go to the Oysters' Benevolent Association, which provided entertainment for bedridden oysters. He became quite an institution in our little community. Boats would take afternoons off to visit him; and Willy, as official guide, made a small fortune in tips. Darwin supplemented the entertainment with his acrobatic display; and in the evenings he and C.J. gave concerts which were enjoyed by all.

In short, we were a great success. The Commander had taken us to his heart and was restless in our absence. In the evenings, when the day's enquiry was over, we would stroll together to the bows and talk over old times. The Commander told me that his whole life had been a kind of enquiry: a search for something worth searching for. As a child he had searched every nook and cranny of the old home; finding many things, but none worth looking for. As a young man he had chosen a political career and explored every avenue: again, without finding his heart's desire. The sailor's life had offered the possibility of endless exploration; and he had explored the seven seas, looking for an eighth. The command of the *Argonaut* expedition was the pinnacle of his ambition; here at last, he thought, was an adventure which must surely reveal something worthy of the search.

And now, he said, in the evening of his life, he had found what he had sought so long. In the collapse of his ambition he had found true fulfilment. Not in achievement, he said, was happiness to be found; not in power, or pride, or success; or any of the worldly things. It was found — here he pressed my arm — in the presence of a loving friend; in a quiet walk to the bows of a ship-wrecked boat; in the laying bare of one's dearest and tenderest secrets.

He would never forget me, he said. In his declining years the memory of myself and my companions would be to him as the warmth of many fires, the light of several suns. And whatever the end might be — however lonely, however fraught with grief — he would go forth on the last and strangest search with the faith of one who knows serenity.

Meanwhile, he said, he was determined to get to the bottom of this date line business. This would be his life's work from now on. It would be his monument to friend-ship. He would not mention, he said, the enormous bene-fit to mariners for ever after, or the fame which would be his if he succeeded. He would say only that this was a labour of love, a humble attempt to serve his friends in their hour of need.

It was with a lump in my throat that I pressed his neck and murmured that we were unworthy of such devotion.

20 *Home at Last*

Our voyage in open boats to California has been described in the official account of the *Argonaut* expedition. I will not repeat it here. Rations ran out, and we suffered a great deal from hunger. When the pangs became acute some of our shipmates looked longingly in Neptune's direction; and a Frenchman named Trottoir spent hours at a stretch brooding over Darwin. But finer feelings prevailed; and Neptune won all hearts by putting his milk into the common pool.

Just when we were at our last gasp we sighted the coast of America. This was superb timing, and the Commander was congratulated on an excellent piece of seamanship. As we passed under the Golden Gate bridge he invited the raft's crew to stay with him; he said that if he remembered rightly he had a house in San Francisco.

A fortnight later we stepped aboard a plane *en route* for England; all except Batters, who had been left behind in dry dock to be scraped and overhauled. He had got into trouble with the port authorities for not being registered as a sea-going craft; but the Commander had pulled a few strings, and a retrospective certificate was issued. The Sufferers' Club of America had sent a committee to report on Batters' sufferings. They were greatly impressed. They agreed that in spite of the breaking of Travelworn's seals, Batters' condition was itself a guarantee of the truth of his story. Photographs and statistics were forwarded to the central office in Geneva, and a claim for two world records was submitted.

D

Our cat report had already been sent to United Nations, and preparations were being made to despatch a scientific and cultural expedition to the island. Willy had sent to the Royal Society a monograph entitled 'The Influence of Radioactive Flying-Fish upon the Oyster-Opening Urge of the Common Cat', intimating that he might be willing to accept an F.R.S. in recognition of his services to science.

We took a warm farewell of the Commander, who had made our short stay in California an unforgettable experience. He said he could never express his gratitude for all we had done for him, and gave us his solemn promise that he would not die until he had solved the date line mystery. At the last moment he broke down altogether. He flung his arms around my neck and had to be dragged away, sobbing, by a squad of airport officials.

We were met at London airport by the usual crowd of reporters and newsreel cameramen. Neptune, who was developing a taste for notoriety, attracted a good deal of attention; but Darwin stole the show by doing a double backward somersault into somebody's glass of beer. He emerged a little tipsy, and made a fool of himself by bungling a simple hand-spring. Willy rang up his lodgings, and learnt with relief that the balance of life had worked quite well, except that a family of fleas had found it necessary to dine out.

And then came the wonderful moment when I was alone at last with my dear wife in our Piccadilly flat. An envelope was lying on the hall floor. It contained a letter from a firm of solicitors. The International Interplanetary Institute was suing me, as financial backer of the *Talking Fish* expedition, for a thousand million pounds.

The case of I.I.I. v. myself was heard before a specially
convened international court in the Albert Hall, London,
the famous Chancery judge, Sir Longful Wittingside, pre-
siding. Sir Grissels Grimley, QC, appeared for the plaintiffs, and Mr Wordsworth Flashington, QC, for the defendant.

The case was opened by Sir Grissels, who said that it
was his intention to show negligence on the part of the
defendant. He would establish that insufficient precautions had been taken by the crew of the *Talking Fish* to
ensure that the Commander of the *Argus* was aware of the
numbers and temperament of the cats.

Stating the case for the defence, Mr Flashington said
that his client denied negligence. He would show that all
reasonable precautions had been taken.

The judge then declared the court adjourned until the
following day. I asked Flashington how he thought we
had done. He said he was satisfied. The first day, he said,
was notoriously tricky; but he thought we had held our
own. I was relieved to hear this; but it was in no enviable
state of mind that I returned home with my dear wife. In
addition to my anxiety about the trial I was worried about
the cats. The balance of life on the island had been completely upset, and although biologists were working day
and night in an effort to find a humane yet practicable
solution, little progress had been made. Supplies of fish
were being rushed in from all directions, and a firm of
salt-cellar manufacturers had converted their plant for

the mass-production of plastic oysters for the kittens to play with. But these were only temporary measures. The exponential law was still operating, and most authorities agreed that the situation was beyond human control.

Next day I was called by Sir Grissels to the witness box. He reminded me that it was the contention of the plaintiffs that on the afternoon of July 20th I had by negligence caused the sinking of the *Argus* in latitude 2° south, longitude 180° west.

'You were aware, were you not," he said, 'of the numbers and temperament of the cats?'

'M'lud,' said Mr. Flashington, rising: 'I object to the question at this stage. My learned friend is attempting to extract an implicit admission that the defendant was present at the scene of the accident.'

'Does my learned friend contend that the defendant was not present?' Sir Grissels asked.

'I contend merely that presence has not been legally established,' said Mr. Flashington.

The judge leaned forward. In his official wig and robes he was an impressive figure. 'The presence or otherwise of the defendant,' he said, 'is a matter of some importance. Perhaps, Sir Grissels, you would be good enough to satisfy our curiosity.'

'Very well, m'lud,' said Sir Grissels. He asked me where I had been on the afternoon of July 20th.

I said I didn't know.

'Come, now,' said Sir Grissels, 'Is it not a fact that on the day in question you were at latitude 2° south, longitude 180° west?'

It was, I said, a moot point.

'You were, were you not, on board the *Talking Fish*?'

'I was.'

'And it was doubtless the practice of the navigation officer of that vessel to work out your position each day?'

'Yes.'

'On the day in question, then, your position was recorded in the raft's log?'

'It all depends,' I said.

Sir Grissels sighed. 'On what, pray, does it depend?'

'It's rather complicated,' I said.

'Be patient with us,' said Sir Grissels. 'We will try to understand.'

'Well,' I said: 'If we had crossed the international date line before the accident, our position on the 20th would be our position on the 19th or the 21st, depending on which way we had crossed the line.'

'Hm!' said Sir Grissels.

'In the second case,' I continued, 'our log would contain no record.'

Sir Grissels passed his hand over his forehead. 'Will you kindly explain to the court,' he said, 'how your position on the 20th could be anything else but your position on that day?'

'It couldn't, of course,' I agreed. 'It's only that the 20th wouldn't really be the 20th.'

Sir Grissels bent to whisper to his junior. The latter shrugged his shoulders. The judge, I noticed, was counting points on his fingers. He had a worried look.

'M'Lud,' said Sir Grissels: 'I request an adjournment.'

'On what ground?' said the judge.

'My wife is expecting a baby,' said Sir Grissels.

When the court assembled next morning the judge enquired after Sir Grissels' baby. Sir Grissels said it had not yet arrived. The judge said he hoped that Lady Grimley was comfortable. Sir Grissels said quite comfortable, thank you, your Lordship, except for a touch of wind.

Mr. Flashington then rose to say that in view of the disclosures of the previous day he wished the legal position of the *Argus* itself to be established. The judge agreed that this was most desirable, and the Commander was called to the witness box. As he was a witness for the plaintiffs I had not been allowed to see him. He waved and nodded to me from the box, and wiped a tear from his cheek.

Under examination by Sir Grissels, he testified that the position of the *Argus* on July 20th, as entered in the ship's log, was latitude 2° south, longitude 180° west.

Mr. Flashington rose to cross-examine. 'You are aware, are you not,' he said, 'of the international date line?'

The Commander said he had heard of it.

'It runs, I believe, through the Pacific ocean along a certain line of longitude?'

'Yes,' said the Commander.

'Which line of longitude is that?'

'180° west.'

'The same line, in fact, as that entered in the log of the *Argus* on July 20th?'

'Yes.'

Mr. Flashington turned to the judge. 'M'Lud, it is the contention of the defence that at the time in question the *Argus* was crossing the date line. This being the case, the date at the stern of the ship was July 20th and that at the bow July 19th or 21st.'

The judge sighed.

'I am, m'Lud, unable to obtain an authoritative decision between the two.'

'And what conclusion do you draw from this circumstance?' asked the judge. His voice had a note of resignation, as of one who had accepted in advance the worst that fate might bring.

'Simply, m'Lud, that on July 20th the bow and the stern were in two different places.'

The judge closed his eyes and took a deep breath. 'And what,' he asked, in a steady voice, 'was the position of the raft on that date?'

'It depends,' said Mr. Flashington, 'on whether it was the 19th or the 21st.'

The judge's pencil snapped in his hand. 'Mr. Flashington,' he said. 'I hesitate to suggest that you are trying to confuse the court; but it appears to my unnautical mind that the position on the day in question would appear in the last entry in the raft's log.'

'That is so, m'Lud.'

'And what, Mr. Flashingon, was that position?'

'St. John's Wood Underground station, m'Lud.'

The judge put his hand over his eyes. His shoulders were seen to shake. Mastering himself, he blew his nose and turned to the plaintiff's bench. 'Sir Grissels,' he said brokenly: 'Is there nothing you can do about this?'

Sir Grissels rose, 'It is possible, m'Lud, that a compromise might be arranged. With your Lordship's permission, I will consult my clients.'

'I should be most grateful if you would,' said the judge. 'Court is adjourned until tomorrow.'

Over a cup of tea in the nearest tea-shop we agreed that the case was going well. Batters said it was as good as over. He had just returned from America and was living temporarily in a treetop on Hampstead Heath. He and Hugo had now returned to normal, and were chafing.

Willy told us that Neptune had recently been working very hard on his pearl, which was now much bigger than it had been.

'Don't let him overdo it,' said C.J.

It was in a mood of quiet optimism that I attended court next day. But it soon became clear that we were not to have things all our own way. Replying to an anxious question by the judge, Sir Grissels said that the baby had still not arrived but the plaintiffs were willing to compromise. They were prepared, he said, to waive the question of the time and place of the accident. He would confine himself to establishing my presence at the event, without specifying when and where it occurred. If it was the contention of the defence that it occurred at St. John's Wood Underground station, he would not contest the point.

Here Mr. Flashington rose, to say that the question of locality was of some importance. He said he failed to see how a ship the size of the *Argus* could possibly have been sunk at St. John's Wood.

The judge said that he agreed with Counsel; the thing was most unlikely. He asked Sir Grissels if he was in a position to prove that the accident did not occur at St. John's Wood Underground station. Sir Grissels called several members of the crew of the *Argus,* who affirmed that at the time of the accident no Underground station had been in sight. He then called the Commander, who testified that I had been present at the time. He told the

court that he had the highest opinion of my character
and was delighted to do this little service for me.

Mr. Flashington rose to cross-examine. 'Where were
you at the time of the accident?' he asked.

The Commander said that he had been in his cabin,
studying navigation.

'So that you could not possibly have seen the defendant?'

The Commander admitted that this was the case.

'In fact, your opinion that the defendant was on the
raft at the time was merely a deduction from the fact
that he was in the water afterwards?'

'That is so,' said the Commander.

'M'Lud,' said Mr. Flashington: 'I can think of seven
different reasons why my client should have been in the
water. I submit that witness has jumped to a conclusion.'

'M'Lud,' said Sir Grissels: 'I can produce witnesses
to prove that the defendant was aboard the raft when it
sailed from Equatorio. I have an affidavit sworn by
Lieutenant Lanyard of the Royal Navy which states that
the defendant was aboard the raft a fortnight before the
accident. The Commander has testified that he was in
the water immediately after it. It is, I submit, a reasonable
inference that he was aboard the raft at the time.'

'The inference is quite unjustified,' said Mr. Flashington. 'I am prepared to prove that the defendant was in
the water at the time when the *Argus* entered the
harbour.'

Sir Grissels grasped the lapels of his gown and drew
himself to his full height. 'I thank my learned friend for
that admission,' he said. 'It will, I think, enable me to
complete my case to your Lordship's satisfaction.'

He called to the box a sailor named Bowsprit, who

testified that a person answering my description had boarded the raft immediately after the encounter and had remained on board while Willy was speaking to the crew of the *Argus*.

'In your opinion,' said Sir Grissels, 'was this person in a position to warn the *Argus* of danger?'

'Yes *sir*!' said Bowsprit.

'*Thank* you,' said Sir Grissels, and sat down eloquently.

Mr. Flashington rose with a kindly smile, as of one who instructs a well-meaning but rather simple-minded beginner.

'Although,' he said, 'there appears to be some degree of doubt as to the day of the month when these events took place, you will no doubt be able to inform us which day of the week it was?'

'Yes *sir*!' said Bowsprit. 'Washing day.'

'Precisely!' said Mr. Flashington. 'Now I want you to tell the court exactly what you were doing at the time in question. Think carefully, Mr. Bowsprit.'

Bowsprit hesitated. 'I were washing me socks,' he said at last. Then he shook his head. 'No I weren't, neither. I'd done them already.' He frowned. Then his face brightened. 'Me smalls!' he said triumphantly. 'I were washing me smalls!'

'Just so,' said Mr. Flashington. 'You are a Leading Seaman, are you not?'

'Yes *sir*!'

'And as such you are no doubt accustomed to doing a job properly?'

'Yes *sir*!'

'You are, in fact, not the kind of person who would spoil a ship for a ha'p'orth of tar?'

'No *sir*!'

'When washing your smalls you would naturally not skimp the job for a ha'p'orth of lather?'

No *sir*!'

'There would be a good deal of lather in your washing-bowl?'

'Yes *sir*!'

'And a good deal on your person?'

'Yes *sir*!'

Mr. Flashington leaned forward. 'In fact,' he said slowly, 'one may assume that, in your habitual attempt to do a good job properly, you were up to your eyes in lather?'

'Yes *sir*!' said Bowsprit proudly.

Mr. Flashington turned to the judge. 'M'Lud, it is the contention of the defence that a sailor with lather in his eyes is in no condition to identify a strange raftsman.'

Sir Grissels sprang angrily to his feet. 'M'Lud, this is mere conjecture on the part of my learned friend. There is not a vestige of proof that witness had lather in his eyes.'

'There is,' retorted Mr. Flashington, 'not a vestige of proof that he did not.'

'If it wasn't the defendant,' snapped Sir Grissels, 'who was it?'

'The defence,' said Mr. Flashington, 'is under no obligation to identify strange swimmers. The burden of proof lies with the plaintiffs. I submit, m'Lud, that identification has not been legally established. There is absolutely no case against my client.'

The judge sighed, and glanced wistfully at a ray of sunshine which had strayed into the hall. 'There is one person,' he said wearily, 'who might settle this matter. I suggest, Sir Grissels, that you call the defendant.'

There was a murmur of excitement as I took my place in the witness box. The judge explained to me that it was his job to get at the truth of this difficult business, and he relied on me to help him. I said I should be glad to do anything in my power. Sir Grissels then asked me if I was the swimmer in question. I said yes, I was. He asked me if I had been on the raft during the critical period. I said yes, I had been. He asked me whether at the time I was in full possession of my faculties. I replied that except for a certain natural excitement and the loss of my pyjama bottoms I had retained all my possessions throughout the entire incident.

After thanking me for my co-operation the judge declared an adjournment. Sir Grissels put his arm round my shoulder and invited me to lunch with him. He said there were some aspects of the case that he would like my advice on. I was about to accept his kind offer when Flashington intervened, saying that he had a prior appointment with me. I said I couldn't remember making one. 'Yes, you do,' he said, and rushed me away quite rudely. Over lunch, he warned me against having anything to do with Sir Grissels; he was a bad character, he said, and would do me nothing but harm.

The afternoon session opened with a statement by Sir Grissels. I examined him carefully in the light of Flashington's remarks, and noticed a certain hardness that seemed to confirm his opinion. I congratulated myself on a narrow escape.

Sir Grissels said that he would now examine the measures taken by me to warn the *Argus,* and would show that they were inadequate for the purpose. He called several witnesses, who gave evidence about my activities during the crucial period. He ended by addressing the judge:

'The actions of the defendant, m'Lud, were thus as follows: While the *Argus* was entering the harbour he went for a swim, and later waved a welcome to the ship's crew. Subsequently, he washed a saucepan and did physical jerks. I submit, m'Lud, that such actions were totally unsuited to the occasion, besides being unworthy of our maritime tradition.'

I confess that I was shaken by this statement. Put like that, it did seem as though I had behaved rather badly. Was I, I wondered, responsible for the whole thing after all?

Mr. Flashington was speaking. 'M'Lud: it is not my intention to claim that these actions would in themselves have been adequate. Fortunately, other things were taking place at the same time. When these other things are taken into consideration the conduct of my client becomes perfectly correct.'

Of course! I thought; I should have seen it for myself. What a brain the man had!

Mr. Flashington now called witnesses from the crews of both vessels. They testified that the following statements had been made by the raft's crew: First: 'You mustn't dock. There are millions of cats on the island.' Second: 'They're operating according to the exponential law.' Third: 'I have proof.'

'I submit, m'Lud,' he concluded, 'that these statements constitute a correct description of the situation. The crew of the *Argus* was adequately warned, and it is with them that the responsibility lies.'

'M'Lud,' said Sir Grissels: 'I cannot concede the adequacy of these statements. The suggestion that a handful of cats could endanger a ship the size of the *Argus* is fantastic. The crew of the *Argus* could not be expected to take it seriously.'

'They had no right to ignore it,' said Mr. Flashington.

'I do not suggest,' retorted Sir Grissels, 'that they ignored it. They rejected it after careful and expert consideration.

'The question is of some importance,' said the Judge. 'We will consider it tomorrow.'

I spent a wretched night. The case was reaching its climax. Soon I might be a pauper, publicly disgraced and saddled with a debt that would take generations to pay off. I worked it out that if I and my descendants had ten children each, all active males who remained unmarried, even my great-great-great-grandsons could scarcely hope to be clear of debt, even allowing for inflation. And if the children weren't all males, or if some got married and had families to support, it became much worse.

There was also the possibility that compound interest would be added to the debt, in which case I didn't see how it could ever be paid. I had a horrifying vision of millions of descendants slaving their lives away for ever as the result of my folly.

To add to my troubles, Willy had telephoned to say that Neptune was very poorly, having worked far too hard, in spite of Willy's warnings. Willy had put him on Jersey milk; but all the goodness seemed to go into the pearl, which was now wonderfully big and beautiful.

In the morning we learnt that Lady Grimley's baby was imminent. Sir Grissels said it was his intention to show that the statements under consideration were inadequate in the circumstances. He called to the witness box a mathematician named Inchingthrottle, who said that the second statement was meaningless. There was, he said, not one, but an infinite number of exponential laws, some of which would indicate that the cats were actually decreasing in numbers. In his opinion the crew of the *Argus* could not have done otherwise than ignore such a statement.

Cross-questioned, Inchingthrottle admitted that the wording of the statement might have been due to Willy's natural excitement, and that if his own comfort had been at stake he would have been inclined to ask for clarification. Prompted by Sir Grissels, he agreed that a ship's crew, whose standards of comfort were somewhat less demanding than his own, could not be expected to exhibit the same degree of scepticism.

Sir Grissels then called a sailor named Sternpost, who shuffled shyly into the box and had to be encouraged to speak up.

'You were, were you not,' said Sir Grissels, 'on the deck of the *Argus* at the time in question?'

'Yus, guv,' said Sternpost.

'You heard the statements which we are now discussing?'

'Yus, guv.'

'What was the reaction of yourself and your shipmates to these statements?'

Sternpost twisted his cap into a tight roll, but said nothing.

'I mean,' said Sir Grissels, 'what did you think of the statements?'

'Well, guv . . . We fought . . . We fought they weren't . . . We fought . . .'

'You thought they were of no nautical significance?'

'That's right, guv.'

'And you, I believe, were appointed spokesman?'

'Come again, guv?'

'You gave the answer?'

'Yus, guv.'

'And what was the answer?'

'You mean,' said Sternpost, 'what did I say to the gentleman?'

'That's right. What did you say to the gentleman?'

'Stick it up your jumper, guv.'

The judge frowned. 'Jumperguv?'

'Jumper, m'Lud,' said Sir Grissels. 'Stick it up your jumper. A nautical term indicating extreme scepticism.'

'Thank you, Sir Grissels,' said the judge. 'I cannot recall meeting the expression in Conrad. But why "jumper"?'

'The origin, m'Lud, is obscure.'

'One would have thought "jersey" more appropriate.'

'Quite so, m'Lud.'

'Could it have any relation to the act of jumping, do you think?'

'I doubt it, m'Lud.'

'Perhaps not. This is interesting evidence. Please continue.'

'Thank you, m'Lud. I wished to establish that the crew of the *Argus* formed a considered opinion of the statements and rejected them in good faith.'

'I think you have made your point, Sir Grissels.'

'I further submit, m'Lud, that the statements have been shown to constitute inadequate warning.'

'In view of Mr. Inchingbottle's evidence,' said the judge, 'I find myself bound to agree with you.'

'Thank you, m'Lud. That completes my case. It has been established that the *Argus* was inadequately warned, and that no blame can be attached to her crew. The responsibility rests entirely with the defendant, whose duty it was to see that the *Argus* was correctly informed. I request a decision in favour of the plaintiffs for the full amount of the claim.'

'I will give judgment after lunch,' said the judge.

I was quite unable to touch my food. I asked Flashington what our chances were, and he said it would do no good to brood; we had all done our best, and nobody could do more than that. The walk to the restaurant was a nightmare. The mid-day editions of the newspapers carried the headlines: NEGLIGENCE PROVED IN ARGUS CASE. People shook their heads as we passed, and the manager of the restaurant said it was a damned shame. The waitress cried over me; and a large dog put its head on my knee and howled. I was getting a fore-

E

taste of the agony to come. My dear wife stroked my hand and pressed Windsor soup on me; but I could only shake my head and fight back the tears.

Willy reported that poor Neptune was in very bad shape. The pearl was getting larger and larger, but Neptune himself was getting thinner and thinner. He was like a creature obsessed; it was as if the pearl had become more important than life itself.

We went back miserably to the Albert Hall, which was crowded with spectators. Women sobbed as I entered, and those within reach patted my shoulder. Even Sir Grissels looked forlorn. He came over to me and said there was nothing personal in all this; he hoped there were no hard feelings. I pressed his hand silently, glad to revise my opinion of him. I asked after his wife, and was told any minute now.

We stood up while the judge made his entrance, then sat to hear the judgment.

'In considering the evidence,' the judge began, 'I have borne in mind the old saying: *Quod hoc sibi vult?*: "What does this mean?" Witnesses have described the actions of the defendant from the moment the *Argus* entered the harbour. I have asked myself what these actions mean; and I have reached a clear and unchallengeable conclusion. We are told that his first action was to go for a swim. From this I can draw one, and only one conclusion. The defendant was unaware of the gravity of the situation. This diagnosis is confirmed by his later actions, which have been attested by the plaintiffs' own witnesses. I cannot conceive that any person in his right mind would behave in this way if he were aware of the true circumstances.

'One may speculate as to the reason for his ignorance. Was it due to secrecy on the part of other members of the raft's crew? Was it due to temporary deafness or a sudden rush of blood to the head? Was it due to simple-mindedness? The question is unimportant. For whatever reason, the defendant was ignorant of the danger; the reason for his ignorance is irrelevant.

'His first intimation of danger comes when one of his companions cries: "You mustn't dock. There are millions of cats on the island." The crew of the *Argus* treated this remark with justified contempt. Can one wonder that the defendant did the same? The second message has been shown to be meaningless; could one expect the defendant's interpretation to be different from that of the crew? And when he heard the third statement, "I have proof", is it not likely that he whispered to himself, even before hearing their verdict: "Stick it up your jersey"?'

'The meaning of the evidence is that the defendant was ignorant of the danger. The corollary is that he is innocent of negligence. I find in favour of the defendant.'

A deafening cheer arose from all parts of the hall. People were on their feet, waving handkerchiefs and throwing each other's hats in the air. Small boys went mad with excitement. Pensioners danced in the aisles.

My wife flung her arms round my neck and kissed me before them all. Everybody within reach was trying to shake my hand.

Sir Grissels was waving a telegram in my face. His wife had given birth to twins.

But my troubles were not yet over. Although I had won
my case the judge gave costs against me. My descendants
were saved from perpetual slavery, but I myself was
heavily in debt. The expedition costs had already swal-
lowed up my capital, and bills were still coming in.
Altogether I owed about twenty thousand pounds. Royalties from my book could not be expected to cover more
than a fraction of this, and most of it was due immediately.

The news from the island was progressively more serious. Helicopter reconnaissance had revealed that the cats
were two deep over the greater part of the island, and three
deep over the remainder. Many cats spent most of their
time in the sea, and a prominent biologist had predicted
that the next generation of kittens would be born with
web feet. If this happened an invasion of the Asian or
American mainland could not be ruled out.

With dreadful pictures at the back of my mind I found
it hard to concentrate on my own financial problems.
None of the others could help me; they were as hard-up
as I was. I sold my car and gave up my pipe, and asked
my wife to economise on my underwear. I even considered taking a job.

Then one day I had a telephone call from Willy. Neptune had asked for me. I hurried round at once, and
found the poor creature very thin and pale, with scarcely
enough strength to hold himself open. It was difficult
to believe that this was the same hardy oyster who had
braved the rigours of raft life with us.

But the pearl itself was a wonderful thing: as big as a cherry and of the most exquisite hue. Willy said it must be worth a fortune. Neptune was still strong enough to hold it up for my inspection, which he did with touching pride. Darwin was sitting beside his friend. Willy said he refused to leave his side. If Neptune did not pull through, he said, Darwin would die of a broken heart.

The faithful creature greeted me with a gentle croak, and I gave him a smile. He said something to Willy, who said that Neptune had a message for me.

'It's about the pearl,' he said. 'He wants you to have it.'

'No!' I said, deeply touched. 'I couldn't dream of taking it.'

'He says he has been working on it for your sake, to help you with your expenses. He says you have always been kind to him, and he can't bear to think of your being ruined on our account.'

'Oh, the dear chap!' I cried, and fairly broke down. Willy said that Neptune didn't want me to be unhappy; wouldn't I smile for him?

Of course I smiled; and stroked his shell. 'Tell him he must get better quickly,' I said. 'Tell him that his health is more important than all the money in the world.'

'He says he will live if he can,' said Willy. 'But if he must die, he will die happy. He says no oyster ever had such friends. He hopes we will remember him.'

I covered my face with my hands.

'He wants you to take the pearl now,' said Willy.

I turned away. 'I don't deserve it,' I said. 'I really don't.'

'Take it,' said Willy. 'He's getting weak.'

I reached out a trembling hand and took the pearl.

'Thank you, old chap,' I said. 'I shall never forget you.'
'Now you had better go,' said Willy.

I took the pearl to Hatton Garden to be valued. The
dealer offered me ten thousand for it. I asked for twenty
thousand and got it. It is now world-famous as the 'Neptune' pearl, and our dear oyster is immortalised.

Meanwhile, he hovered between life and death, nursed
devotedly by Willy and Darwin. The summer days short-
ened and the melancholy autumn days took their place.
Nature was preparing for her winter sleep; and it seemed
that our little friend would fall asleep too. The other
animals appeared to sense his condition; they were less
lively than they had been, quieter in their ways and more
considerate of each other. Tannhäuser would sit motion-
less for hours, with a large tear in each eye, like an age-old
monument of grief.

The humans, too, felt the pathos of his decline. There
was not one of us who, reaching out in sympathy to the
gallant creature, was not softened and matured. We, too,
grew kinder to each other, and more understanding.
Faults were forgiven, and unsuspected virtues discovered.
We loved each other for our very imperfections. In the
serene hour of a turquoise twilight we would come together in silent communion, and feel ourselves close to the
heart of some great mystery.

The sad day came when Willy summoned us to the
bedside. Neptune, he said, was very weak; he could not
last the night. We sat around his bowl in quiet vigil, talking in whispers and watching for a change. For the first
time, he did not recognise me; it nearly broke my heart.

In the still dark hour before dawn no sign of life was
visible. Willy said it was all over.

And then he rallied. Somewhere within that wasted frame a spark of obstinate vitality flickered. When the first finger of day touched the edge of his bowl, he moved in his shell, as if the light had wakened him. Poor Darwin, who had been sobbing at his side, sprang to attend him. A radiant smile transformed the frog's tear-stained face as he turned to us and croaked his message.

Willy translated. 'Neptune wants to know where the funeral is. He'd like to see a smile or two around here.'

Returning home after a hilarious breakfast, during which Willy got over-excited and had to be laid flat, I realised that during the crisis I had hardly given a thought to the cats. Buying a newspaper, I found to my great relief that things had taken a turn for the better. The cats, who at the zenith of their powers were doing things at five hundred times the usual speed, had begun, for no known reason, to slow down. Perhaps they were tired.

The rest is history. Having slowed down to normal, the cats began to breed chiefly males, with just an isolated female here and there to keep them from getting self-centred. The population fell rapidly, a balance of life was quickly established, and the island shows every sign of becoming a cats' paradise.

Some weeks later we had a grand reunion in Willy's attic. Willy's F.R.S. had just come through, and he had invited us to celebrate the occasion. The crew of the *Talking Fish* were all there, of course: Hugo and Batters, still chafing; C.J., as plump as ever and almost as brown; Willy, at his wits' end to find room for us all; and myself. At my request the Commander had been invited; he had made an immediate hit with the animals, and was entertaining several of them in a corner. Tannhäuser had taken a great liking to his trousers.

A space had been cleared in the middle of the table; and here Darwin and Neptune were installed in their bowl of milk, which was laced with lemonade for the occasion. Neptune was now fully recovered and as fit as ever he had been. He had started work on another pearl, using a process which he had invented himself and which he thought might revolutionise the industry. He and Darwin were still the best of friends; but something of the old liveliness had returned to their relationship, and they were not above playing practical jokes on each other. When I arrived Darwin was making grabs at the pearl, and getting himself well nipped.

I was now a complete convert to Darwinism, and Willy had been trying to teach me frog's language. I had, consequently, a rather sore throat, which was not improved by having to inhale the fumes from Batters' pipe. He was smoking what he called 'Covent Garden Mixture', which he said was the most successful of his experiments. I was

quite willing to believe it. He and Hugo were still sceptical about Darwin; but, as I said to Willy, some people
will disbelieve anything. When he forgot to chafe, Batters
was in high spirits; his two world records had been confirmed, and he had appeared several times on T.V. A well-
known shipbuilding company had offered him an enormous salary for a series of experiments on underwater
encrustation.

While we were evacuating several small families in
order to prepare a meal, the Commander told us of the
progress of his enquiry. He was, he said, as far from a
solution as ever. It had been pointed out to him that with
the imminence of space travel the date line question had
become even more important than it had been in the past.
Space travellers far from the earth would be unable to go
the other way round to avoid the line. He foresaw some
nasty interplanetary incidents if the matter were not
cleared up soon. He was now convinced that a theoretical
solution was impossible. He intended to try an experiment. He would cross the Pacific, marking off the days
carefully on a calendar, and compare the result with the
local calendars at his port of arrival. He would start as
soon as he had found a suitable calendar. We congratulated him on his initiative and wished him luck. Hugo said
he would come with him, provided that the voyage were
done in a cricket pavilion. They shook hands on the deal,
and Willy presented them with a broken cricket bat. He
apologised for the state of the Commander's trousers; but
the latter said he had always preferred shorts.

After the meal we took a democratic vote to decide who
should do the washing up. While I was doing it Willy
made a recording of the others' voices, beginning with a
duet by C.J. and Darwin, who rendered their Eisteddfod

piece very nicely, in spite of Darwin's difficulty with the Welsh *Ll*. The Commander followed with a very moving song entitled 'Dearest Friends of Long Ago', which was almost too much for me. Hugo and Batters did a rather silly thing called 'The Rugby Player's Romance'; and Willy finished up with 'All Creatures that on Earth Do Dwell'. I refused to sing; but I made a sincere speech which I thought expressed our feelings rather well. Hugo seemed to think so, at any rate, for he remarked that I took the Christmas cake.

When Willy played the recordings back a rather queer thing happened. Before the duet started we heard a strange squeaking noise which lasted for several seconds. Willy identified it as a quarrel between Hengist and Horsa, which was the last thing he had recorded on the previous spool. C.J. at once became excited. He asked Willy a number of questions and tinkered about inside the machine. He made an experiment with two spools, and reproduced the same effect. He turned to Willy.

'Silly fellow you are,' he said. 'Inductive feed-back you have got.'

'Have I?' said Willy, alarmed. 'Is that bad?'

C.J. told him that when the switches were in a certain position the last sounds on a spool became impressed on the first portion of the next.

'And that is where your talking fish came from,' he said.

It was as clear as daylight! The word 'blum-blum' which was heard on the fish recording had been transferred from the end of the Buburup recording. The search for the talking fish had been a wild goose chase.

Willy had gone pale. He was, I knew, undergoing a spiritual crisis. His self-respect was at stake. This was the moment when he must reconsider his philosophy and decide whether he still believed in himself.

He sat for some time, frowning, his hands clasped between his knees. We watched in silence.

Suddenly he took a deep breath and struck the arms of his chair.

'No!' he said.

He looked at each of us. 'No! I don't believe it! Inductive foodbasket or not, that recording was genuine! I'd stake my reputation on it.'

I seized him by the hand. 'Bravo, old chap!' I said. 'You've found yourself!'

'I'll find the talking fish,' said Willy, 'if it's the last thing I do.' He turned to the Commander. 'If you'll have me, I'll join your expedition!'

'Delighted, old fellow,' said the Commander. 'Now, if we could only persuade C.J. and Binder to come, too . .'

'I wish I could,' I said. 'But I have my book.'

'My Eisteddfod I have,' said C.J. 'And a good thing, too.'

Thereafter the party became uproarious. Hugo and Batters took it into their heads to give a display of competitive gymnastics, including items like hanging by their teeth from the mantelpiece and turning somersaults on the table. Darwin outdid them both with one hand behind his back. At some point in the proceedings I received a severe kick on the head, and had to retire into a corner. The Commander came with me and held my hand. Later, Hugo organised a football match – amphibians versus mammals – in which Tannhäuser, as goalkeeper for the former, proved impassable. All the animals entered into the fun – including the family of fleas, who made themselves sick by overeating; and at the end of it Darwin made a neat little speech in which he thanked the humans for their sportsmanship. Willy replied on our behalf; and the evening closed on a note of mutual affection.

It was in the early hours that we said good-night. Everybody was yawning. Neptune was one huge yawn; he had had the time of his life. At the door I turned and waved to him; and Darwin croaked in reply. 'Neptune would like to have a talk with you sometime,' said Willy.

'What about?' I asked.

'Democracy,' said Willy, closing the door.